meribel

les 3 vallées

first edition 2004

written and edited by
Isobel Rostron & Michael Kayson

Qanuk Publishing & Design Ltd
www.snowmole.com

the snowmole guide to **méribel les 3 vallées**
first edition 2004

published by Qanuk Publishing & Design Ltd
45 Mysore Road London SW11 5RY

printed by Craftprint, Singapore

ISBN 0-9545739-4-3

A catalogue record of this book is available from the British Library.

snowmole does not accept any advertising or payment, and the guides are written free from any bias.

The contents of this book are believed correct at the time of printing. As things can change, errors or omissions may occur. The publishers and authors can accept no responsibility for any loss, injury or inconvenience sustained by anybody using information or comment contained in this guide.

contents

4 how to use the guide
5 how to use the maps
6 explanation of icons

text

introducing méribel

10 overview
13 seasonal variations
14 quintessential méribel

getting started

18 planning your trip
20 getting there
25 getting around
26 accommodation
36 lift passes
39 skis, boots & boards
41 lessons & guiding

the skiing

48 overview
54 saulire (map d)
58 tougnète (map e)
60 mont du vallon (map f)
63 courchevel 1850 (map b)
67 courchevel 1650 (map a)
69 la tania, le praz & 1550 (map c)
72 st. martin de belleville (map g)
74 les menuires (map h)
76 le masse (map i)
78 val thorens & maurienne (map j & k)
82 suggested days
84 off-piste & touring
86 events & activities

the resorts

90 overview
92 méribel centre & mussillon
100 the suburbs
102 méribel village
104 les allues
106 mottaret
112 activities
114 children
116 seasonnaires

the a-z

120 tour operators
122 directory
128 glossary
130 index

maps

route & resort maps

fc méribel centre & mussillon
21 self-drive
23 fly-drive
27 hotels
93 méribel centre & mussillon eating out
97 méribel centre & mussillon après-ski & nightlife
101 the suburbs
103 méribel village
105 les allues
107 mottaret

ski maps

individual sectors & ski area overview ➥ inside back cover

how to use the guide

How much you enjoy your winter holiday depends on a variety of things. Some you cannot influence - you can't guarantee sunshine, good snow, or your flight landing on time... but most things should be within your control. With the majority of ski holidays lasting just a week or less, you don't want to waste time trying to find a good restaurant, or struggling with an overgrown piste map. The snowmole guides are designed with 2 purposes in mind: to save you time by providing essential information on the operation of the resort, and to help you to make the most of your time by giving insight into every aspect of your stay.

The guide is not intended to be read from cover to cover. After the introduction to the resorts, the guide is split into 4 distinct sections - getting started, the skiing, the resorts and the a-z - so you can dip into the information you need when you need it. Some information will be useful to you beforehand, some while you are in resort and some while you are on the mountain.

getting started deals with the basics: how to get to the resorts, how to get around once you're there, and your options when buying your lift pass, renting equipment and booking lessons or mountain guides.

the skiing gives an overview of the mountains and the ski area, information on the off-piste, and a breakdown for beginners, intermediates, experts, boarders and non-skiers. The ski domain has been divided into digestible chunks and for each there is a detailed description of the pistes and lifts.

the resorts covers the best of the rest of your holiday: for each of the resorts, there is a series of reviews on where to eat and where to play as well as general sections on what to do when skiing isn't an option, facilities for children and tips for seasonnaires.

the a-z comprises a list of tour operators, a directory of contact details (telephone numbers and website addresses) and information from accidents to weather, a glossary of terms used in this guide and in skiing in general, and an index to help navigate your way around the guide.

how to use the maps

The guide also features a number of maps, designed and produced specifically for snowmole. While the information they contain is as accurate as possible, some omissions have been made for the sake of clarity.

route maps — show the journey to the resort from the UK, from relevant airports or the roads within the area surrounding the resorts.

resort maps — one for each resort (showing pedestrianised zones, main buildings, and where relevant, car parks, train lines, and road names).

ski maps — each individual area has its own contoured map. These show details such as the lifts, pistes and mountain restaurants. The contours have been mapped to fit an A6 page - few ski areas are perfect rectangles. They are accurate only in relation to the pistes they depict and should not be used for navigation. Pistes are shown only in their approximate path - to make the maps as user-friendly as possible some twists and turns have been omitted. The ski maps are grouped together at the back of the book to make them easy to find and refer to - even with gloves on. There is an overview map on the inside back cover that shows the entire ski domain and how the individual ski maps fit together. The back cover has a flap, which is useful as a page marker for the individual ski maps. In the chapter on the skiing the overview map is reproduced in miniature alongside the descriptions of the individual sectors.

explanation of icons

review headers

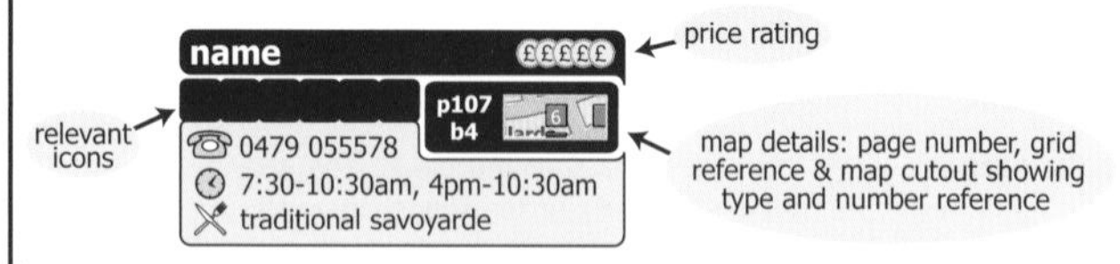

basic details

- telephone number
- fax number
- email address
- website address
- number of beds
- office address
- opening hours
- food type

ski school icons

- ski lessons
- snowboard lessons
- child-specific lessons
- disabled skiing
- specialist courses
- G - guides available

hotel icons

- on-site rental store
- shuttle bus

others

- food available
- take away
- live music
- tv
- internet station(s)
- bar
- terrace

town maps

buildings

- tourist office
- lift pass office
- post office
- supermarket
- cinema
- church

travel specific

- parking
- covered parking
- bus stop
- route specific bus stop

commerce colour coding

- savoyarde restaurant
- restaurant
- cafe
- take-away
- bar
- nightclub
- hotel

route maps

 - train line & station

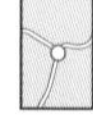 - main road & town

 - country borders

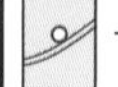 - motorway & town

 - airport

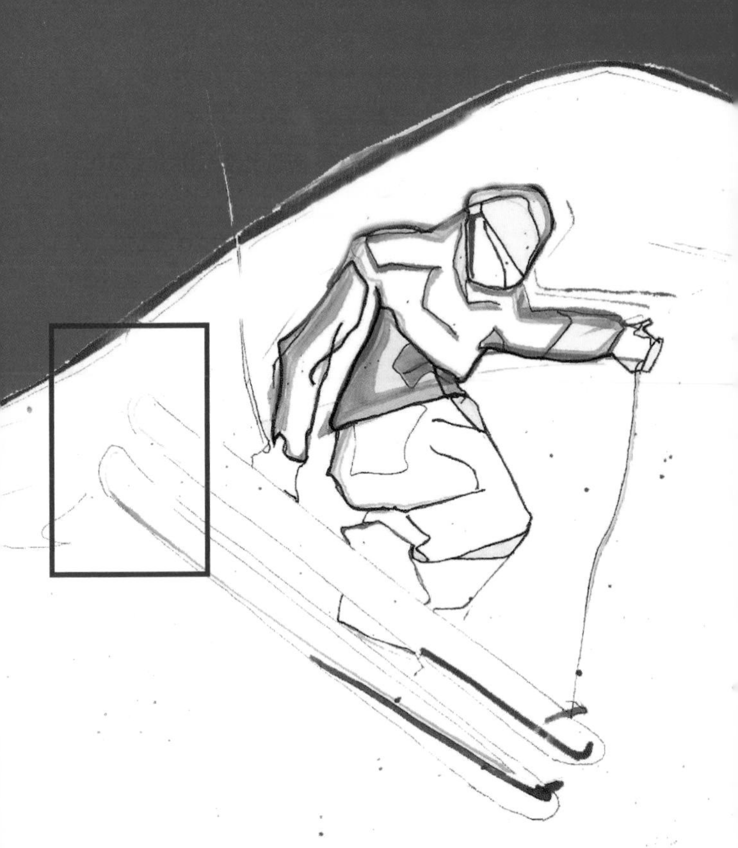

introducing méribel

Méribel, very belle, lies in the Vallée of Les Allues at the heart of the 3 Vallées, one of the world's best known ski areas. Despite being in France it has a very English heart, the result of being the vision of the British Colonel Peter Lindsay. On discovering the valley in 1936 he decided to create a Savoyarde Davos. Strict rules of building were applied - only timber, stone and slate were used and only low-rise buildings were allowed. In the main these rules are adhered to today - though the resort has since sprawled up much of the mountainside, its architecture is very much in harmony with the alpine surrounds. The skiing has probably got something to do with its success as well and it's not surprising more visitors arrive each year and many return. Imagine a ski resort and the picture in your mind wouldn't be too far from Méribel - very belle indeed.

The Vallée of Les Allues is home to several villages and hamlets, 14 of which fall under the ski resort umbrella of Méribel. Skiers may find themselves staying in the Centre or in one of the 'suburbs' - L'Altiport, Le Rond-Point, Le Belvédère, Le Morel and 1600, which lie on a series of tiers above the Centre (1400m-1710m) - or one of the satellite villages of Les Allues, Mussillon or Méribel Village. The purpose-built resort of Méribel-Mottaret lies further (south) up the valley - towards the Mont du Vallon peak. The spa town of Brides-les-Bains is also joined to Méribel by the Olympe gondola, a 30 minute ride from La Chaudanne (the name given to the main hub of lifts in the Centre).

Unsurprisingly given its origins, over 35% of Méribel's visitors today are British - and many of the chalets are English-owned or run. And as a third of the 15,000 or so Americans who ski in France stay in Méribel, this ensures the domination of the English language. The locals will tell you that in recent years the French are gradually filtering back, enough to give the resort quite a cosmopolitan feel.

Where you stay will affect how convenient you find the resort - though most of the suburbs and satellite villages have enough of an infrastructure on which to survive, the main restaurants, bars and shops are in Méribel Centre. Accommodation consists largely of privately owned chalets - more than in any other European resort - while the bulk of the hotels are 3 stars.

Après is concentrated in Méribel Centre, with pockets of fun elsewhere - such as Le Rond-Point (at Le Rond-Point), La Tsaretta in Les Allues and Le Lodge du Village in Méribel Village. But unless you're staying in one of those places you probably won't bother to visit. Unsurprisingly the après generally has a very British flavour - in terms of the staff, the drinkers and the drinks available.

It is fortunate that the Italians invented pizza, as Méribel's restauranteurs seem to have adopted it as their signature dish. Consequently eating out is neither too imaginative nor too expensive - though there are a couple of places with higher culinary aspirations where it is possible to blow the holiday budget. And mountain restaurants (as anywhere) offer questionable value for money.

snapshot

highs...
sunny slopes somewhere throughout the day
skiing convenience
at the heart of the 3 Vallées
quantity of pistes
good for beginners

and lows
a skiing bottle-neck
as French as fish and chips
dispersed village with muted nightlife
traffic jams/bottlenecks
poor bus service

For a long time the 3 Vallées was the world's biggest ski area - the valleys have been linked since the 1950s. In 2004, the linkage of the skiing above Les Arcs to the skiing around La Plagne and the creation of the Paradiski area brought a young pretender to the throne. Yet in terms of connections and skiability, the 3 Vallées is still king. A pedant would note that the 3 Vallées should be renamed the 4 Vallées, thanks to the recent addition of lift links from the Maurienne valley to Val Thorens in the Vallée of Belleville. Whatever, the 3 Vallées offers skiing for every standard - but it is predominantly about covering miles and the stats are impressive. The lift system (though not the lift pass system) is one of the most efficient and modern in the world - and it is constantly being up-dated. Though the majority of visitors to Méribel are happy to stay on the piste, there is enough off-piste in the 3 Vallées to justify a book about it - see 'Les 3 Vallées Hors pistes - Off piste' by Philippe Baud and Benoit Loucel.

The commercial core of the valley is **méribel centre** at 1450m - the largest and most diverse of the resorts in the area. Its central square is home to the post office, the tourist office and the main ESF office, while the bulk of the shops, restaurants, bars and off-slope facilities lie along its 3 main wooden-façaded streets. The resort-level lifts and main lift pass office are found at La Chaudanne, at the lower end of the village, where you will also find the Parc Olympique and the Tremplin commerce complex. Centre has good access to the ski area, both immediately above the village and in the other valleys. It also hosts the majority share of the après scene, though 2 popular venues - Dick's Tea-bar and Pizza Express - are found in **mussillon**, the small road-side hamlet that you pass through on your way to the Centre. Here you will also find many of the chalets run by UK tour operators.

On the Saulire side, the road above Centre winds its way through the resort's suburbs - first **morel**, **1600**, **le plateau**, followed by **le rond-point des pistes**, **le belvédère** (an enclave of luxury chalets and 2 Club Med hotels) and leading ultimately to **l'altiport**. It is a 10 minute bus ride from Le Rond-Point to Centre. The road through the suburbs is lined with chalet and apartment accommodation and the occasional bar, shop, restaurant or supermarket - and the lower pistes down from the Saulire peak run past the edges of the development.

For somewhere more charming and true to the origins of the region, head back down the valley to **les allues**. Similar to Courchevel's Le Praz, the village retains a distinctive Savoyarde feel and as it has a year-round population (of English and French) it feels as if it exists for reasons other than skiing. **méribel village** is also separate from the main resort - on the road to La Tania and the Courchevel valley - and is where new meets old. While remnants of the original village remain, it is overshadowed by a relatively new MGM chalet-hotel development.

At 1700m-1800m, **mottaret** is the highest of the villages and, in contrast to Les Allues, exists solely for skiing and as a result is fantastically convenient - nearly all accommodation is ski in/ski out. Mottaret is made up of 2 hamlets - the older Le Laitelet and the newer Le Châtelet - joined by a central hub of commerces and pistes at the bottom of the resort. Though they are purpose-built and functionally designed, because it adheres to the same architectural rules as its lower altitude sister it is better in appearance than most. But you can't quite ignore the slightly multi-storey feel, and as there are no trees to soften the view it is can seem rather bleak. That said, Mottaret has the best links to the skiing of all the villages - both Courchevel and Val Thorens are within easy reach.

Predicting the weather in the mountains is always difficult. The lower villages are generally a little bit warmer and a little less snowy than uppermost Mottaret, which tends to be more at the mercy of alpine winds and blizzards.

temperatures

Temperatures are easy to generalise - December and January are usually the coldest months, with things warming up through February, March and April. Don't be fooled by appearances though - it will often be colder when there is a cloudless, blue sky than when snow is falling. Temperatures can range from as low as -10°C at resort level (and colder up the mountain) on the coldest days to as high as 20°C late on in the season when the sun is shining.

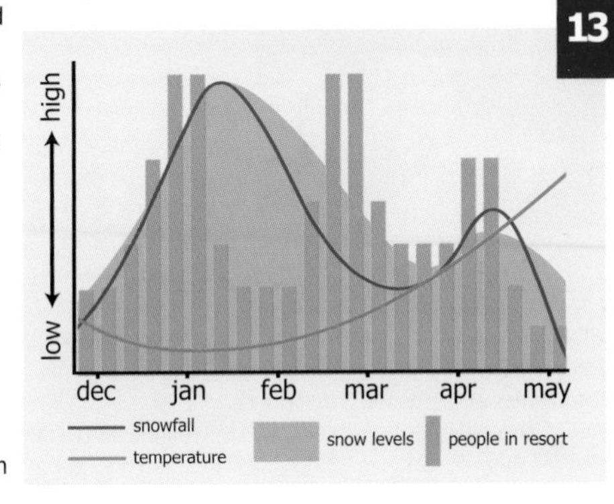

snowfall

When and how much snow falls varies from year to year, but trends do emerge. The snow is at its best on the lower slopes during January and February - later on in the season it tends to disappear soon after falling. Upper slopes can be at their prime in March and April after enough snow has fallen to establish a good base. Snow cannons have their work cut out to keep the lower slopes open at the beginning and end of the season.

volume of people in resort

Like other major resorts, the peak weeks are Christmas, New Year, the English and French school half terms (the middle to end of February) and Easter (when it falls early in the year). During these times, accommodation prices are at their highest and everything gets booked up months in advance. February in particular is hectic when skiers appear like families of rabbits, meaning long queues, fully booked ski schools and less choice in the ski shops. In contrast some weeks in January can seem unbearably quiet. Being some distance from a major airport, Méribel is not an obvious choice for weekenders.

Ski resorts are as varied as DNA. But what makes Méribel Méribel? To have a quintessential time...

surround yourself in wood

If you're not staying in a chalet, you're almost missing the point of Méribel - few resorts do them in such abundance, or with such a range. And you are not confined to a particular location - there are chalets from Les Allues to Mottaret and even the small hamlet of Chandon is getting in on the act. The top end of the range includes the beyond luxurious Ski Lodge Boreale, which has facilities that many of the hotels can only aspire to - a swimming pool, spa tub, champagne on tap and staff to cater for your every whim. If your budget doesn't stretch as far as the price tag, there are plenty of other more than comfortable options.

learn some tricks

Méribel was one of the first European resorts to embrace the concept of snowparks - and one of the few to do them really well. The valley has two - the Moonpark at L'Arpasson (moonpark.net) on the Tougnète side of the valley (for which you can buy a separate lift pass) and the Plattières Park on the right of Mont du Vallon. There is a park above Les Menuires, 1 above Val Thorens, 4 in the Courchevel valley, a snowcross in Les Menuires and a boardercross in the 4th valley - definitely time to get some air.

speak english

No words of wisdom about how a little of the local lingo goes a long way. In fact, quite the opposite. Over the years, Méribel has become an English resort for English people - so if you are hoping to practise your French you may be disappointed. Chances are if you order your drink in French you won't be understood. If you do want to search out the local scene, Le Saint Amour in Centre has a lovely French hostess, Chez Kiki in Morel stays true to its roots and Le Plantin just beyond Méribel Village is where you are most likely to be able to join in a chorus of 'Allez Les Blues'.

become a groupie

Méribel is the Alpine equivalent of Madison Square Gardens - so many groups play live music in the valley that it almost needs a gig guide. Those serious about joining their following shouldn't miss Wednesday après at the Rond-Point, where skier's favourite Shibbolith have a regular slot. Bands also play frequently at La Taverne and the Doron Pub in the Centre - just remember to talk about Toast, Super U, Blue Funkt, Patchwork and Foreplay rather than Coldplay and Keane.

go for gold

As a host to the 1992 Winter Olympics Méribel has some truly world class facilities. You can live out your own sporting dreams at the Parc Olympique at La Chaudanne, or on the slopes you can test yourself on the women's downhill - the long black from the top of the Olympic chair. Though there is no podium at the bottom you can reward yourself in the bar with some liquid gold.

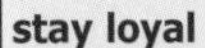

stay loyal

Méribel has a loyalty scheme for regular visitors. 'Mérifique' offers members a number of advantages: a priority queue for buying passes; discounts on various resort activities; regular newsletters; competitions; and private tours of the changes made to the ski area at the beginning of each season. Membership forms are available from the tourist office and lift pass offices - so you can really feel like you belong.

take the family

La Plagne in Paradiski a few ridgelines away may pride itself on being the 'family resort' but Méribel comes a close second. The resort is well equipped to deal with ankle biters, with kindergartens at La Chaudanne, Le Rond-Point and Mottaret, as well as an English-run nanny service. There are plenty of gentle slopes around the Altiport and the chairlift there can take the family up the mountain in one sitting and still leave room for their friends.

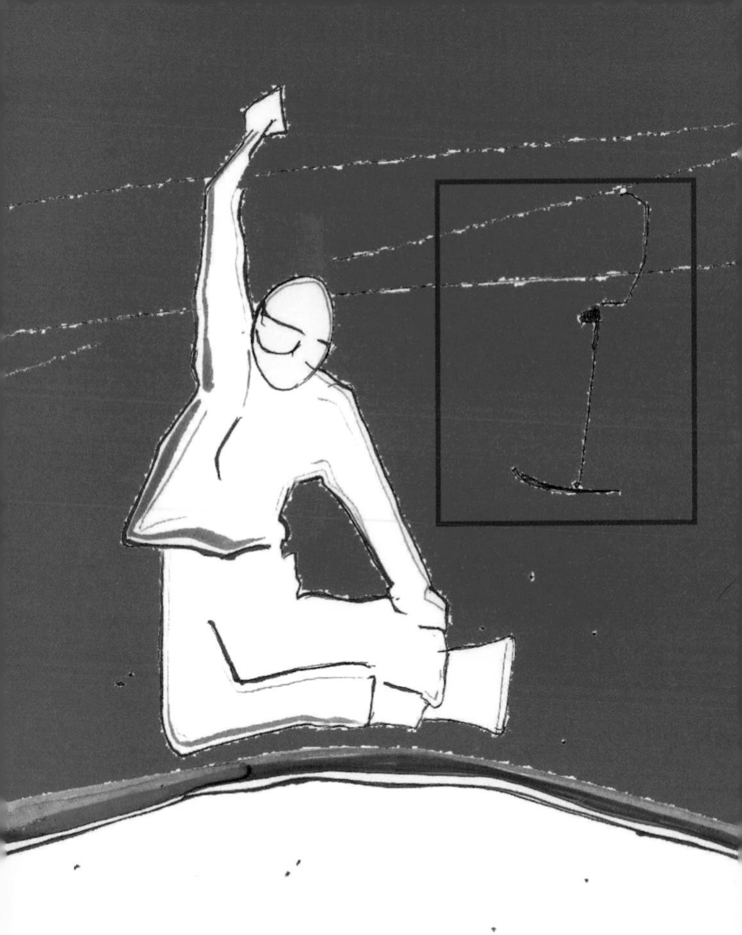

getting started

Once you know you want to go to Méribel, you need to decide how you want to get there. Traditionally, most skiing holidays are booked though travel agents or tour operators, but with the advent of cheap flights, DIY holidays are becoming more popular. There are pros and cons to both.

18 package

The theory behind package holidays is that all you should have to think about is getting from the top of the slopes to the bottom. The core of every package deal is convenience - though it comes wrapped in all kinds of paper. Ski companies fall into 2 types: large mainstream operators, and smaller more specialist ones. The mainstream brand offers ready-made holidays, where everything is already planned and you take it or leave it. Trips with smaller companies can be more expensive, but tend to be more flexible and many tailor the trip to your exact requirements. Alternatively, if you don't want to be restricted to a single operator, a travel agent will have access to a selection of holidays offered by several companies.

Mainstream companies only run week-long trips, from Saturday to Saturday or Sunday to Sunday - giving you 6 days on the slopes and 7 nights in (or on) the town. They charter their own **flights** - making the holiday cheaper - but you have little option as to when or from where you travel. Smaller ski companies give you greater choice - many specialise in long weekends for the 'money-rich, time-poor' market, with departures on Thursday evenings and returns on Monday evenings. This gives you 4 days skiing for 2 days off work... but the real advantage is their use of scheduled flights, so you can pick the airport, airline, and when you travel.

With a mainstream company, your **transfer** to resort will be by coach, with others who have booked through the same company. You may have to wait for other flights, and on the way there may be stop-offs in other resorts or at other accommodation before your own. Because you're travelling at the weekend the journey tends to take longer. With a smaller company you may transfer by coach, minibus, taxi, or car depending on how much you've paid and the size of your group. And if you arrive mid-week, the transfers tend to be quicker.

What your **accommodation** is depends entirely on whom you book with. Some companies only offer apartments, some specialise in chalets, some operate in specific resorts... the limiting factor is what's in the brochure - though if you want to stay in a particular place, a more specialist company may try to organise it for you.

In **resort** some companies offer a drop-off and pick-up service from the lifts, which is a huge advantage in sprawling Méribel. But the main benefit of a package holiday is the resort rep. From the moment you arrive to the moment you leave, there is someone whose job it is to ensure your holiday goes smoothly... or that's the theory. More than likely your rep will sort out lift passes and equipment rental. Some will organise evening activities and be available for a short period every day to answer questions. Most are supported by an in-situ manager who deals with more serious issues. The more you pay for your holiday, the better your rep should be. The best are service-oriented French speakers... but it is difficult to recruit hard-working, intelligent, bilingual people to work for next to nothing. If you want to know what - or who - to expect, ask when you book.

DIY

If you DIY, you have more control over the kind of holiday you take and what you pay. But as you have to make all the arrangements, you'll need more time to plan the trip.

Several **airports** are within transfer distance of Méribel - so you can fly to whichever one has the most convenient flights for you. The major airports are Geneva and Lyon St. Exupéry, which are serviced by the major airlines (BA, Air France or Swiss) as well as some of the budget options (such as Easyjet and bmibaby). Some of the budget airlines also fly to the smaller airports of St. Etienne, Chambéry and Grenoble. The cheapest flights are normally from London, and the earlier you book the cheaper it will be. The airlines accept reservations for the upcoming winter from around June or July. Some chartered airlines such as Monarch or Thomas Cook may also have a limited number of seats for sale. For **transfers** to Méribel you have a variety of options (➥ getting there). If you don't want to fly, the excellent European motorway system makes **driving** to the Alps surprisingly easy. Getting there by **train** is also an option.

On a DIY trip the choice of **accommodation** is endless - you are not restricted by brochures or company deals... however the easiest way to book a chalet or an apartment is through a company or website offering accommodation only, such as Interhome or ifyouski.com. You can liaise with the owners directly if you can find their details, but this is often difficult. For hotels you might be able to get a discount off the published price by contacting them directly. For more information on hotels, chalets and apartments ➥ accommodation.

In **resort** is perhaps where the difference between DIY and package is most noticeable. There is no rep on hand so you have to buy your own lift pass, organise your own equipment rental... but this can have its pluses: you can be sure that you get exactly the right type of pass and you can choose which rental shop you use.

How long it takes to get to Méribel is something of a lottery - the turn-off from the motorway is in Moûtiers, which is also the turn-off for the other resorts in the 3 Vallées and is en route to the Espace Killy and the Paradiski ski areas. As such it can be a bit of a slog on transfer day, particularly making your way through Albertville, which needs a bypass road like you need your mobile phone.

All contact details for the transport listed can be found in the directory.

overland

The most common starting place for any journey by **car** to the Alps is Calais. You can reach Calais from the UK via the **eurotunnel** or by **ferry**. Then by car it is just over 665 miles (just over 950 kms) from Calais to Méribel - a journey that can be done in about 11 hours. The journey from Calais takes you east of Paris, through Reims to the mustard town of Dijon (about two-thirds of the way if you want to make an overnight stop along the way). From Dijon head down past Bourg-en-Bresse to Lyon where you head east towards Moûtiers and the Méribel turn-off. There are 2 *péage* (toll) stops on the route south through France, for which you collect a ticket as you enter the motorway and hand it in as you leave. Expect to pay around €50 in total - you can pay with cash or by credit card. The French Gendarmerie operate a queuing system on and off the stretch of motorway between Albertville and Moûtiers - which although frustrating is quite effective and prevents you from having to rely on your traffic survival skills. Although Méribel Centre is only approx 18kms from Moûtiers (where you leave the motorway from Geneva), the winding road up the mountain turns it into a 30 minute drive - and more if there is traffic or snow.

There are 2 alternatives to the standard **ferry** crossing to Calais. The first is with Norfolkline to Dunkirk - often quieter (and less prone to lorry strikes!) than the Calais services. The second is SpeedFerries.com - a new fast ferry service to Boulogne. SpeedFerries sells tickets on a similar basis to the budget airlines - the earlier you buy, the less you pay.

If you like the open road but not the driving, Ski Méribel offers a door-to-door **sleeper coach**, from London and Dover to Moûtiers and Méribel. Eurolines also runs **coach** services from the UK to Moûtiers, from where you can transfer up to the resort. Once you get to Moûtiers you can get to your resort by **bus**. Transavoie operates 2 regular services from Moûtiers every day - 1 service runs to Mottaret, stopping in Les Allues, Méribel Village, Mussillon and Méribel Centre (La Chaudanne) along the way while the other runs to the Altiport, stopping in Méribel Village, Méribel Centre, La Chaudanne, Plateau and Le Rond-Point. The services run

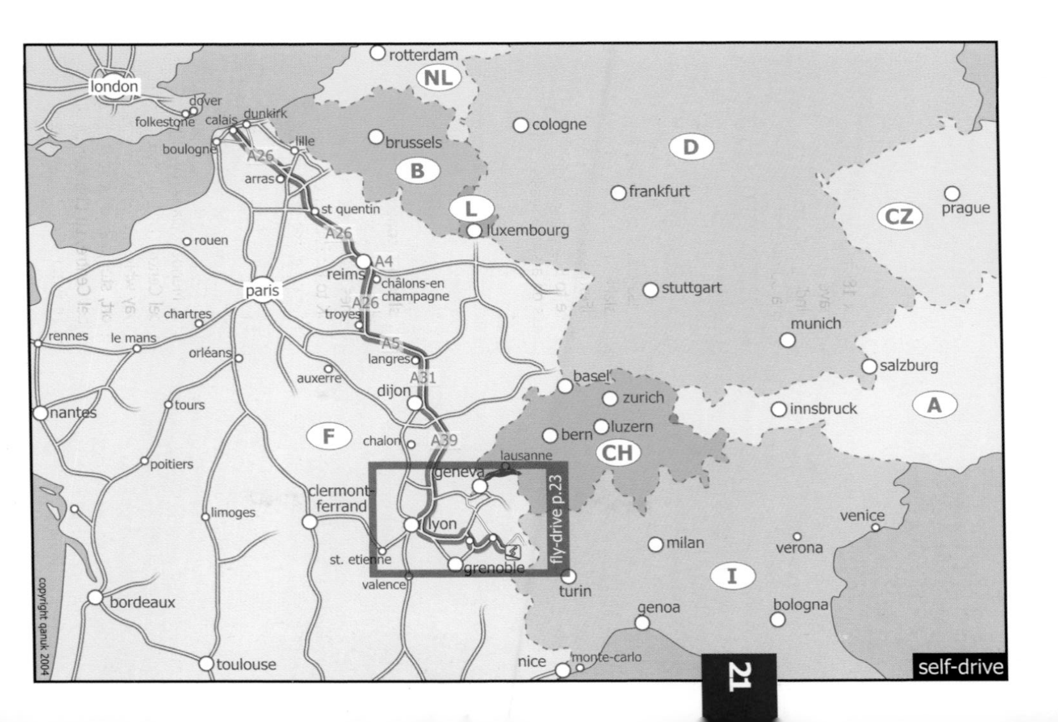
london
dover
folkestone
calais
dunkirk
boulogne
lille
A26
arras
st quentin
rouen
rotterdam
NL
brussels
B
L
luxembourg
cologne
D
frankfurt
CZ
prague
A4
reims
châlons-en champagne
paris
A26
troyes
chartres
rennes
le mans
orléans
A5
langres
auxerre
A31
dijon
stuttgart
munich
salzburg
basel
zurich
innsbruck
A
nantes
tours
F
chalon
A39
bern
luzern
CH
lausanne
poitiers
geneva
fly-drive p.23
clermont-ferrand
limoges
lyon
venice
milan
verona
st. etienne
grenoble
I
valence
turin
bordeaux
genoa
bologna
toulouse
nice
monte-carlo
copyright qanuk 2004

more frequently at weekends. All return journeys must be booked 48 hours in advance at the tourist office. A one-way ticket costs €11 - children aged between 4-12 years travel half-price.

Travelling **by train** to the Alps gives you more time in resort - 8 days instead of the usual 6 - a particularly excellent service if you live in London. The stop for Méribel is Moûtiers. All train services from the UK become full months in advance so be sure to book well ahead.

The **snowtrain** is the classic way to travel by train to the Alps. You check in at Dover on Friday afternoon, take a ferry to Calais where you board a couchette (a train with sleeping compartments) and travel overnight, arriving in the Alps on Saturday morning. The return service leaves the following Saturday evening. Another option is the **eurostar overnight** service, which leaves London Waterloo (with some services stopping in Ashford, Kent) on Friday evenings. You travel directly to Paris, where you change onto a couchette to travel overnight, arriving in the Alps on Saturday morning. The return service leaves on Saturday evening. The **eurostar direct** service runs during the daytime, leaving London Waterloo on Saturday mornings and arrives in the Alps on Saturday evenings. The return trip departs on Saturday evening. If you can't get onto the Eurostar services, the French intercity service (**TGV**) is an option. The journey from Paris (Gare de Lyon or Austerlitz) to Moûtiers takes anything from 5-8 hours. There are a few services every day - some of which are direct, some of which require on 1 changes. To get to Paris, you can either fly or take the Eurostar

The Transavoie bus service from Moûtiers train station to the Méribel resorts and Mottaret is timed to coincide with major train arrivals including the Eurostar and Snowtrain.

by air

From the UK, you can fly to 2 international airports - Lyon St. Exupéry (180kms) and Geneva (135kms) - though the greatest number of flights fly to Geneva. There are less frequent air services to Lyon St. Etienne (240kms), Grenoble (160kms) and Chambéry (100kms) (➥ planning your trip).

transfers

One way to get to Méribel from your arrival airport is by **car**. You can hire one at any of the airports - book over the phone, on the internet, or when you arrive at the airport. Your car will have the necessary equipment such as an emergency triangle, but you will need to specifically ask for snow chains and a roof box if you want them.

It takes an average of 3 hours to get to Méribel from Geneva - though on a

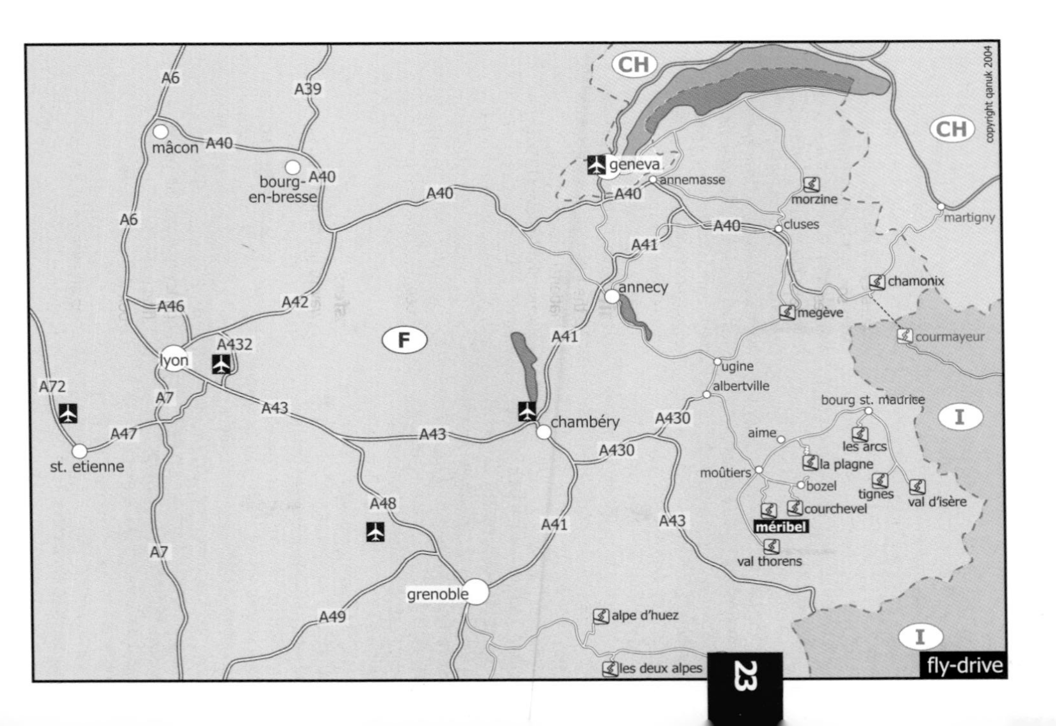
CH
CH
F
I
I
geneva
annemasse
morzine
cluses
martigny
chamonix
courmayeur
megève
annecy
ugine
albertville
bourg st. maurice
aime
les arcs
la plagne
moûtiers
bozel
tignes
val d'isère
courchevel
méribel
val thorens
chambéry
grenoble
alpe d'huez
les deux alpes
lyon
mâcon
bourg-en-bresse
st. etienne
A6
A39
A40
A41
A42
A43
A46
A47
A48
A49
A7
A72
A430
A432
copyright qanuk 2004

good run this can be as little as 2, and as many as 6 if the traffic is bad or you are travelling during a peak week. The journey by road from Chambéry takes about 1 hour, and from Lyon 2½, though as for Geneva double it (and more) for travel during peak weeks or at weekends.

You can get to Moûtiers easily by **train** from Lyon (3 hours), Grenoble (2.5 hours) and Chambéry (1.5 hours) - there is no direct service from Geneva, which makes it a more tiresome option. The SNCF have a desk in the tourist office in Méribel (open Tuesdays-Saturdays 9am-12pm, 3pm-7pm).

Société Touriscar runs a **bus service** from Geneva (€100 return) to Méribel for the duration of the season. A similar service is run by Transavoie from Chambéry and by Satobus Alpes from Lyon. Seats for all services must be reserved at least 48 hours in advance. If you don't want to drive or take public transport, a number of companies run **private minibus transfers** from the airports direct to your accommodation. Services vary from a simple pick up and drop off to the provision of welcome packs and food and even champagne during your trip. There are a number of services including ATS, Alp Line, Mountain Transfers and Alpine Cab. All of them take online bookings, either via email or direct through the relevant website. ATS run shuttles from Geneva, as well as private transfers. Most of Alp Line's services run from Geneva though they will pick up from any of the French airports (this costs more). Mountain Transfers pick up from Geneva, Chambéry and Lyon St. Exupéry and also Moûtiers. Alpine Cab is the luxury option, picking up from Geneva, Grenoble, St. Etienne and Lyon. 3 Vallées transfers is a Courchevel and Méribel specialist offering transfers from the airports and Moûtiers. **taxi** is an expensive alternative - a one-way trip from Chambéry airport costs just over €200 while from Geneva or Lyon it is closer to €300. Or if you really want to splash out you can always transfer by **helicopter**.

The various villages are well signposted on the way up the mountain - the first you pass through is Les Allues. Further along a right turn takes you to Méribel Centre and the suburbs and a left to Méribel Village (and if you follow the road to its end, to La Tania and Le Praz). The turning (a left) for the suburbs is just after the road-side village of Mussillon. The road to the suburbs is a head-spinning round of switchbacks, so make sure you have a tight grip on the steering wheel and decent tyres on the ground. From Le Rond-Point the road continues left to the Altiport and right to Belvédère. A one-way system operates in Méribel Centre, which can cause snarl-ups around the town square. Fortunately you can get to Mottaret without having to navigate this - a ring road runs below the Centre, passing by La Chaudanne. The spread-out nature of the resort means that only those skiers staying in the Méribel Centre are unlikely to use public transport. If you don't have a car you can walk or catch a bus or taxi. If you decide when you get to Méribel that you need a car, you can hire one (➥ the directory).

Your opinion of getting around **on foot** will depend upon where your accommodation is. Those staying in Méribel Centre will probably enjoy the short walks between accommodation, skiing and après, whilst those in the suburbs will laud the free **bus service** (*navette gratuite*) that links them to the Centre. This is free with a lift pass and runs along 4 routes, 8am-11:30pm The frequency of the bus depends on the route - the most regular being bus no.1, between La Chaudanne and the Altiport (and other stops in the suburbs). Bus no.2 runs from La Chaudanne to Belvédère, bus no.3 links La Chaudanne and Méribel Centre to Mottaret and no.4 links Les Allues and Méribel Village to the Centre and La Chaudanne. Reliability and regularity are not strong points of the service and during the getting home rush hour it can be so overcrowded as to be unbearable. There is also a daily service in the early evening between Centre and the Courchevel valley (with stops in La Tania, Le Praz, 1650 and 1850). If you're allergic to public transport, you can always get a **taxi**. Though more expensive it is an essential means of transport for those staying beyond the reaches of the free bus or for those who stay up later than the free bus does. You can ask at the tourist office for a full list of taxi drivers.

snapshot

from méribel centre by road to
mottaret - 10 minutes
courchevel - 40 minutes
la tania - 10 minutes
val thorens - 1 hour
les menuires - 40 minutes
val d'isère - 1 hour 30 minutes
bourg st. maurice - 1 hour

At the end of the day on the slopes, you probably won't mind where you rest your head. But when planning your holiday, you might want to put more thought into where you stay. Because of the sprawling nature of the resort, it is a good idea to read the small print as to where your accommodation is actually located - so you don't find that your 'Méribel' is actually Les Allues, when you were hoping to be in the thick of the action. And with 35,000 beds to choose from it's easy to get confused about where yours will be.

Whichever part of Méribel you choose for your holiday you are likely to stay in a chalet or an apartment. The few hotels that there are in the valley are concentrated in Centre itself and around Le Rond-Point. Chalets are what Méribel does best, from luxury to budget, with more than in any other resort in the Alps. A lot of traditional chalets are available either through the tour operators or as private rentals.

To encourage holidaymakers to book direct the Méribel tourist office has its own reservations desk (t 0479 005000, i reservations@meribel.net), which maintains a large database of all the accommodation available in Méribel at any particular time. They will search it according to your requirements - though it is a good idea to be quite specific about what (and where) you want. This system also offers various packages that include one or more of lift passes, ski hire and tuition - and overall they tend to work out a little cheaper than if booked separately. Accommodation is normally available from mid-December until late April, with availability best at the start and end of the season.

hotels

Méribel's hotels come a poor second to those over the ridge in Courchevel. The widest choice is in the 3* bracket - a pleasant selection of comfortable hotels that should leave you quietly happy. You can count the number of 4* hotels on 1 hand, though if the top end of the range is what you are looking for you should consider elsewhere - the word 'luxe' does not appear.

specifics

During the peak weeks of Christmas, New Year, and the February half-terms, the hotels will only take week long **bookings**, either Saturday to Saturday or Sunday to Sunday. Outside of these weeks, it is possible to book a shorter stay, although you are more likely to get a long weekend if you book last-minute.

In France the number of **stars** a hotel has is directly connected to its facilities. Things like room size and whether there is a lift dictate how many stars are awarded. Where the rating system can be misleading is in the divide between 2* and 3*. Often a room in a 3* hotel will not be noticeably different to a much cheaper room in a hotel with 1

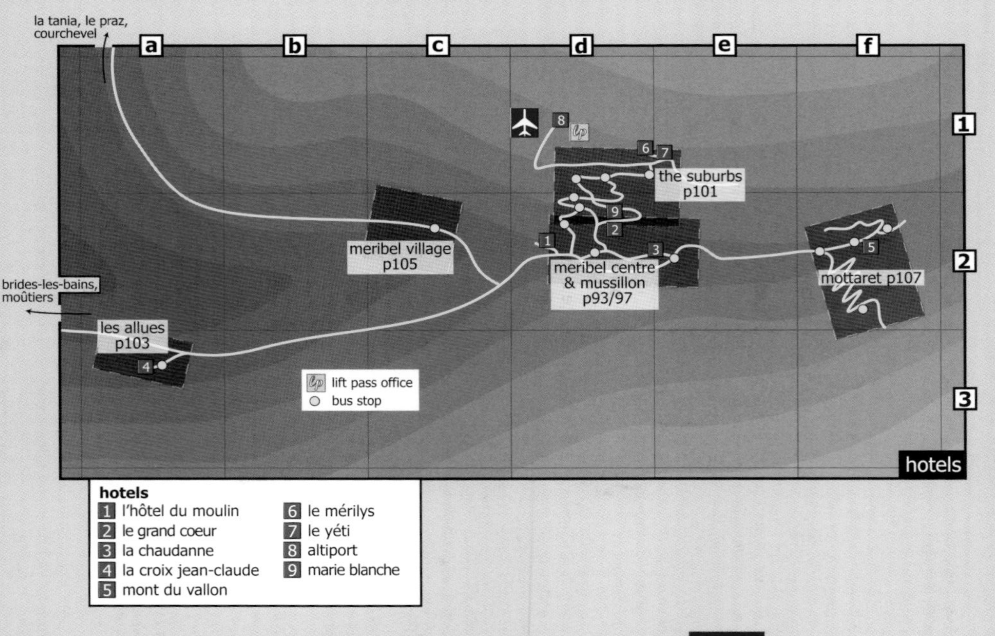

hotels

1 l'hôtel du moulin
2 le grand coeur
3 la chaudanne
4 la croix jean-claude
5 mont du vallon
6 le mérilys
7 le yéti
8 altiport
9 marie blanche

less star. Nonetheless the 4* hotels are generally the most comfortable and have the widest range of facilities.

Every front-of-house employee will speak **english**, so unless you have a quibble with a cleaning lady you will be able to survive with no French at all. But hotels are where you will notice a difference if you can speak in French. Staff are more likely to be more sympathetic to questions (or complaints) if you make the effort to communicate with them in their language.

A number of the hotels are **ski-in/ski-out** - particularly those around Le Rond-Point, Belvédère or the Altiport - and broadly speaking when you run out of piste you won't have far to walk to get home, and you're bound to pass a bar or two on the way. A disadvantage of staying up in the suburbs is that the bulk of the shops, non-hotel restaurants and night life lie lower down the hill in Centre and La Chaudanne.

prices

The price ranges are approximate figures for a double room per night in high season, including tax but not service.
luxury over €300
mid-range €150-€300
budget under €150
In addition most hotels have low, mid and high season price brackets, (determined by demand) - and some charge even more for the festive periods of Christmas and New Year. All hotels accept most credit cards.

snapshot

for...
as cheap as chips - l'hôtel du moulin
ski to the door - yéti
peace & quiet - marie blanche
luxury - le grand coeur
middle of the action - la chaudanne
french - la croix jean-claude
lodge-style - mont du vallon
snowy surrounds - adray télébar
a good all-round package - mérilys

<< luxury >>

The only luxury option in Méribel and reassuringly the best. As you would expect the facilities are excellent, the furniture and décor are thoughtfully chosen and the attention to detail very French. Le Coeur is also one of the best located hotels for the slopes - the back door leads onto a path to the Doron blue piste, which runs down to La Chaudanne and means you can ski (or at least pole) in and out - and it is a snowball's throw from Centre. Service is pleasant without being obsequious and if the hubbub of the resort gets too much, you can relax in the hotel's extremely comfortable lounge at the end the day. Though not cheap, the food served in the restaurant earns its pricing and you can enjoy your meal while enjoying the lovely view over the resort.

The Mont Vallon is the luxury option in Mottaret. A rustic lodge at the bottom of Châtelet, it is well placed for all the amentities of the resort, and its own facilities are pretty good too - and include a well-equipped gym, squash court, swimming pool and a jacuzzi. Rooms are comfortable and spacious though some suffer from being a little close to the flight path of the Plattières gondola - not for those who want a lie-in, though it can inspire you to get out of bed and onto the slopes. Its brasserie, Le Schuss, has a fantastic slope-side spot and an extensive menu that goes beyond the usual choices, but which is probably the most expensive lunch option in the resort.

<< mid-range >>

Though the Mérilys only has 3 stars after its name, it is the undisputed star of the cluster of hotels found at Le Rond-Point. Located on the edge of the forest, the pine trees make for charming surrounds. The inside is charming too - pleasantly decorated throughout with wood (beams and walls) and white walls, and the rustic look is completed with dried flower arrangements and sheepskin throws.

Only breakfast is served but a number of the other hotels close by serve dinner to non-residents - and there is a bar if liquid will suffice. It is also conveniently close to the slopes - less than a 5 minute walk. Apartments are available as well, with 2-5 rooms which are thus ideal for families or groups. Children will enjoy the games room and parents the sauna and gym - all in all the Mérilys has something for everyone.

The trio of hotels and apartment accommodation - La Chaudanne, L' Eterlou and Le Tremplin - ("Les 3 hotels de Méribel") have the edge over their competitors in many ways. Like many of the 3* hotels they are slope-side (or close enough), but unlike many they are also within a minute's walk of the main hub of lifts at La Chaudanne as well as in the thick of the shop, bar and restaurant action. The shared leisure facilities (in La Chaudanne) of swimming pool, sauna, hammam, jacuzzi, and squash courts seem to merit a 4th star. La Chaudanne is the only one you can truly ski in and out of - but that's a minor grumble. Service too is friendly and though the rooms don't seep luxury they more than adequately do the job they were designed for.

The Marie-Blanche sits down a quiet road above the Centre - from which it is a 15 minute (downhill) walk. More of a chalet than a hotel in its style - with a roaring log fire in the lounge area and lovingly chosen artefacts - the feel is consequently more intimate than in some of the purpose built hotels elsewhere in the resort. The restaurant serves good food - during the day lunch can be taken on a south-facing terrace - so you have no real need to leave and can make the most of the quiet land scenic location.

If you hadn't guessed by the name, the Altiport hotel is next to the resort's airport at the top of the winding road through the suburbs. Though the slopes and lifts of the Altiport ski area are within a 2 minute walk - making it convenient for the skiing - the surrounding area has little else to offer, and so is only recommended for those seeking peace and quiet. The hotel's Blanchot restaurant has a good reputation for both dinner and lunch - for the latter a buffet is served on the terrace on sunny days.

The Yéti ties with the Mérilys for the award of most charming hotel at Le Rond-Point. Right on the edge of the Doron piste it is truly ski in/ski out. In a similar vein to the Mérilys, wood is put to good use throughout - and plenty of windows make the most of its slope-side vantage point. All rooms - ranging in size from double room to duplex apartments - face south or west and have a mountain view and balcony.

<< budget >>

The small 'Windmill' on the fringes of Mussillon is the best budget option in the valley and it is within striking distance of Centre. It is also the top choice for those who like pizza and late nights - Pizza Express is just across the road and Dick's Tea-Bar is only a small stumble further.

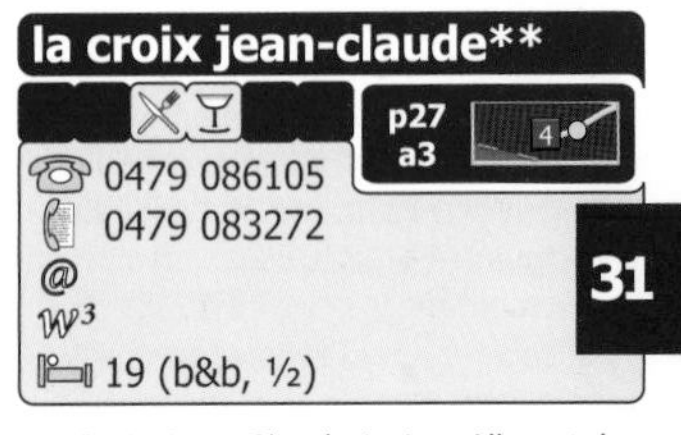

La Croix Jean-Claude in Les Allues takes the prize for the most French hotel in the valley - both in style and attitude. Located on the main road through the village, rooms are traditional and simply furnished, the staff are from 'round these parts' (rather than seasonnaires) and you fully expect to find a member of the Resistance living in the attic. The restaurant has a bigger reputation than the hotel and serves food at both lunchtime and in the evening - and for the latter it is a good idea to book.

and the rest

Those looking for all-inclusive need look little further than Club Med (i clubmed.co.uk) who have 3 hotels in Méribel. The 4*s - **le chalet** (t 0479 232823) and **l'antarès** (t 0479 232823) - are in the Belvédère area, while the 3* (**l'aspen park** (t 0479 005177)) sits between the Mérilys and Yéti hotels by Le Rond-Point. All have an extensive range of leisure facilities and lie in close proximity to the slopes. For slopes on all sides the **adray télébar** (t 0479 086026, telebar-hotel.com) sits in the middle of the Doron blue piste. A budget option in Méribel Centre is **le doron** (t 0479 086002) - though as this is above Le Pub it is best suited to those who enjoy their après and intend on a few late nights. Another hotel at Le Rond-Point, the 2* **l'orée du bois** (t 0479 005030, i meribel-oree.com) will take bookings from Monday to Friday during low season. In Mottaret the **alpenruitor** (t 0479 004848, i alpenruitor.com) on the Laitelet side is under the same management as the 4* Les Airelles in Courchevel. Other options in Mottaret include **les arolles** (t 0479 004040, i arolles.com) and **le mottaret** (t 0479 004747, i eurogroup-vacances.com) - both of which are 3*.

chalets

Chalet holidays cater for those who want to stay in a more relaxed setting, but don't want to fend for themselves.
If you choose to stay in a chalet your can book with a tour operator or hunt out a privately run chalet. There are few chalets in the Centre, more in Mussillon, Les Allues and increasingly so in the small hamlet of Chandon.

tour operators

Méribel's popularity as a destination for families makes it a prime location for tour operators, and accordingly almost every tour company in existence offers some kind of holiday to a Méribel resort

- more British tour operators offer chalet accommodation in Méribel than in any other resort. Whereas in some resorts chalets range from the basic and functional to the plush and luxurious, Méribel has more than its fair share of the latter. That said, the typical package is the same as anywhere else - bed, breakfast, afternoon tea and on all but 1 night of your stay an evening meal with wine. You will be looked after by at least 1 English chalet host and normally a resort manager. Tour companies will also organise flights and transfers, and some offer discounts for groups booking up an entire chalet. Because of the spread-out nature of the resort, some of the operators offer a minibus service to and from the lifts at the beginning and end of the day. Very few chalets are ski in/ski out. The rule of thumb is that the more you pay, the better you can expect the quality of everything to be. But unless you book the whole place you take pot luck with your fellow guests - it can be a war zone or the beginning of a beautiful new friendship - but at least you know you all like snow.

independents

Méribel has almost as many independently run chalets as the Chamonix valley. They generally fall into 2 camps - those where you are left to your own devices and those that offer a similar deal to the big tour operators, though with some you can decide how much the owner gets involved. They can be hard to track down, although the internet is a good place to start - some owners have their own websites or list their chalets on sites such as **ifyouski.com**. **interhome** also maintains a huge database of privately-owned accommodation in Méribel. The website **chaletfinder.co.uk** allows you book direct with the owner of the property, while the English run **chaletgroup** (i chaletgroup.com) has information on a number of privately

run chalets in the valley. The tourist office produces a helpful booklet containing details of all the private landlords offering accommodation (chalets and apartments) in the Méribel valley. This gives you contact details for the chalet/apartment owner so you can deal with them directly.

résidences

Résidences are effectively large and well appointed apartment blocks, such as you might find flanking the south side of the Thames in London. Most have their own gym, bar, swimming pool and sauna - but they are basically self-catering accommodation with a nice foyer. The apartments house between 2 and 8 people, often in 2 or 3 adjoining rooms (some have up to 6) which will be kitted out with full kitchen facilities and bed linen - all you need to bring is some food.

One of the best is the MGM-owned **les fermes de méribel-village** in Méribel Village (t 0825 063000, i residences-mgm.com). Apartments are contained in 6 chalet-style buildings - though no meals are served, the entrance lobby and the swimming pool with its picturesque view onto the nearby slopes wouldn't look out of a place in a 4* hotel. The **chalet les pistes** (t 0479 086083, i lespistes.com) at Le Rond-Point isn't far behind in terms of style and facilities and has the advantage of an on-site snack bar, for when you can't face the kitchen. Pierre et Vacances also has a presence in the valley including the **belledonne** (t 0479 083165, i pierreetvacances.com). In Mottaret the Odalys owned **domaine du soleil** (t 0158 565656, i odalys-vacances.com) at the top of Laitelet offers reasonable rates in reasonably good quality accommodation ranging from studios to 3 bedroom apartments. It has its own bar and the facilities of Le Hameau lie within easy reach.

apartments

Ski apartments are typically compact and bijoux, and while Méribel has its fair share of them, Mottaret has even more. Though Mottaret has traditionally catered for the budget end of the market, recent additions (particularly in Châtelet) are aimed at a more discerning market. The close proximity of Mottaret's older apartments to the pistes - taking ski-in, ski-out to a whole new dimension - make up for what they lack in size. Some in fact are so close to the piste that you may be kept awake at night by the snow cannons and piste bashers at work. In the older builds an apartment for 4 is generally 2 rooms (a bedroom and living room), with 2 guests sleeping on a sofa-bed and are equipped with the bare essentials - don't expect to arrive to a stocked fridge or even a loo roll - while the newer kind may have a microwave. In all you will be expected to clean it at the end of your stay, or pay the rental agency to do the same if they decide your dusting and hoovering skills aren't up to scratch. You can find apartments from 1 of 3 main sources: accommodation agencies, UK tour operators and the tourist office's list of private landlords. As property (sales as well as lettings) is big business in this part of the Alps, Méribel has enough estate agencies to rival a London suburb. In Méribel, **méribel agence** (t 0479 086208, i meribel-agence.com), **maeva** (i maeva.com), **agence des neiges** (t 0479 086521, i meribel-neiges.com) and **latitude 1700** (t 0479 004406) all deal with lettings, as do **agence de la saulire** (t 0479 004189, i meribel-neiges.com) and **agence du mottaret** (t 0479 228656, i gsi-immobilier.com) in Mottaret. Apartments are on the face of it the cheapest place to stay - but when you add in the price of food and meals out, you can pay more overall than you would pay for a hotel or chalet. However if you can live like a sardine and stay disciplined about what you spend on food, it can be cost-effective. Prices vary depending upon whether it is high, mid or low season. As a guide, a short-term let for a mid-grade apartment with 2 rooms (4 beds) costs approximately €1000 in peak weeks and €500 in low season. Some apartments are available on a long-let if you want a place for the season. The demand is high so make sure you book early. The Méribel tourist office are due to launch a grading scheme for apartments, under which accommodation will be awarded a number of 'hearts', according to the standard of its facilities, which will help visitors to more easily find accommodation of the required standard and encourage owners to upgrade the quality of their property. Until then a better way to get the idea of size and layout is to ask to see a floor plan and what the square footage is. And to take some of the hassle out of apartment living the English-run **chaletfood** (book online at chaletfood.com) will do your supermarket shopping - food, drink and household items, and deliver the shopping to your door. Various standard packs are available, and special requests are catered for. Prices are competitive with the resort supermarkets.

camping

There is a *caravaneige* ("Le Martagon" t 0479 005629) with 15 spaces in Le Raffort, a small village a little further up the valley from Les Allues.

a cheaper option

The spa town of **brides-les-bains** (t 0479 552064, i brides-les-bains.com) at 600m is small and picturesque and located at the bottom of the Les Allues valley. You can rarely ski to it, but it is well linked to the ski area by lift - the Olympe gondola. Accommodation in Brides is a mixed bag of hotels and apartments, all at considerably lower prices than further up the valley. Add to that the good facilities (a health club, a cinema, the area's only casino), and numerous restaurants and shops) and you have the ideal destination for a cheaper winter holiday. A number of the mainstream tour operators run holidays to Brides, or those specialising in tailor-made programmes may be able to organise something for you.

Higher up the hill the **chalet jeunesse et famille** in Méribel Centre is a good option for families on a budget (t 0479 086039, i jeunesse-et-famille.com) - similar to a youth hostel, it has 34 rooms and is well equipped to deal with children and parents alike.

Once you've arrived in Méribel and found where you're staying, there are a few things to do before you can get onto the slopes. For many people, long queues and language barriers make this the worst part of the holiday. Starting with lift passes the following pages take you step by step through the process and how to survive it.

Despite the up-to-date lift system, the lift pass is one of the most archaic - leaving the 3 Vallées in the dark ages compared to other resorts. You need to show your pass at the entry to most lifts on the mountain, which on a cold, windy day can be tiresome. And this will continue to be so, as there are no plans for a hands-free system. The price is high too for Europe - for 6 days the change you'll get from a €200 note will only be enough for a croissant. But compare it to the price of the North American resorts or break the cost down per kilometre of piste, and it's a veritable bargain.

méribel or three vallées?

If you opt for a 3 Vallées pass you can ski the whole of the domain, from Courchevel to Orelle. It is the most expensive option but the least complicated - and if you buy one for 6 days or more you get a 1 day pass for either the Espace Killy or the Paradiski ski areas. You have to collect a lift pass at central ticket office of each resort. If you buy a pass for 5 or more days

snapshot

useful information
lift passes available for mottaret, méribel, the méribel valley and the 3 vallées
photo required for passes of 3 days or more
snowpark pass available
a family pass includes children up to the age of 18
1 day skiing in espace killy or paradiski with a 6 days (or more) 3 vallées lift pass

you can then buy an extra day at a lower rate than a 1 day pass. It is also possible to buy a 3 Vallées add-on if your original pass is for 2 or more days. The pass for the Méribel valley is cheaper, but only marginally so. And the choices don't end there. As the lifts in the Méribel valley are managed by 2 lift companies (Méribel Alpina and Méribel-Mottaret (S3V)), it's not just about 1 or 3 valleys, but also about the upper or lower ends.

Any lift pass allows you to use the bus service that runs around Méribel for free. All passes over 3 days or more require a photo. None of the lift passes include the Olympe gondola from Brides-les-Bains - this costs €9.

handy to know

You can **buy** your passes from the main Méribel Alpina lift pass office at La Chaudanne - open Mondays-Fridays

8:45am-5pm, Saturdays 8:45am-7pm and Sundays 8:45am-5:30pm. The main S3V lift pass office is at the bottom of the pistes in Mottaret, next to the tourist office. Both offices have a separate queue for those wanting to buy just a day pass. There are also smaller offices at Le Rond-Point, the Altiport and in the satellite villages. If you have any questions about lift passes, what the conditions are like or which areas are open, Méribel Alpina runs a small information chalet at La Chaudanne. Both the Méribel Alpina and S3V lift companies offer a **pre-booking service**, either by post or online (i meribel-alpina.com, i s3v.com) - a good way to avoid the queues or convenient if you are not staying near a lift pass office. You can have your passes delivered to your hotel, arrange to collect them at the tourist office, or from a priority line at the lift office itself. If you are travelling with a tour operator they usually collect lift passes for you. You can buy any pass for any number of days. It is more cost effective to buy a pass valid for all the days you plan to ski, as the overall cost decreases as the number of days increases. So if you plan to ski for 6 days it is cheaper to buy a pass for 6 days than a day pass for each day. Lift passes for the next day can be bought from 3:30pm onwards the day before you want to ski.

half-day passes can be bought for the afternoon from 12:30pm - ideal for late risers. Children **under 5** and adults **over 72** can use the lift system for free - though you still need to get a lift pass to prove your age claim. Children aged between **5-13 years** and 'seniors' between **60-72 years** qualify for a discount on proof of age. Children's lift passes can also be bought as part of a ski school package. A **family** of 2 parents with 2-5 children aged 5-18 years qualify for a family pass (for just the Méribel valley or the 3 Vallées) - this saves about 20% on individually bought passes, particularly as discounts for children's passes are only available for those aged 13 or under. In certain weeks a family pass for 7 days can be bought for the price of 6 (check on t 0479 005000, i les3vallees.com).

There are a number of free lifts in the valley: in Méribel the Côtes draglift, the Altiport drag and in Mottaret the Chalets gondola and the Doron drag. The **mini ski** pass is ideal for **beginners** who have exhausted their use of the free lifts. Available for just the afternoon or 1 day, this gives access to the lifts up to, in and around Le Rond-Point, the Golf chair from the Méribel Village and the Morel chair from Morel.

The **pedestrian** lift pass gives access to gondolas and cable cars in the Méribel and Courchevel valleys. Or pedestrians can can buy a ticket for a single trip on a the chosen gondola or cable car the trip down is free.

Depending on the snow, an **early season** lift pass is available (normally in the first 2 weeks of the season) - for 6 days this is €100 cheaper than the full price for a normal 6 day pass and gives access to any ski area open. In the last week of the season (again snow dependent), the **spring** ski pass is about €50 cheaper than full price.

The **option** pass is a good choice for those who will spend more than a week in the area. This gives you 12 days of skiing for whenever you decide. The only drawback is that you must go to the office that sold you the lift pass to get a valid ticket for the day you want to ski - so not very convenient if you intend to stay in Courchevel for 1 week and Méribel for another. However if you plan to visit Méribel or the 3 Vallées several times during the season, buying a **season** pass can be the most cost-effective approach.

You can buy a **snowpark** pass just for the Moonpark above Méribel, good for 3 days of your choice - this allows you to use the Plan de L'Homme chairlift to get there and the Arpasson draglift alongside the park.

You can buy additional **insurance** when you get your lift pass - for a small extra charge on top of the lift pass price. Known as **carré neige** (t 0479 311080, i carreneige.com) this covers all costs of search, rescue, ambulance and reimburses you for lift passes over 3 days (accident, loss, theft, serious illness or bad weather) and lessons (over 3 days), medical expenses, legal aid insurance, interruption of ski lift service (over 1 day). Insurance is required even for free passes. Any passes which are found are deposited at the central lift pass office at La Chaudanne.

There has been a renaissance in the previously hassle-tastic ordeal of getting your equipment sorted. A number of the rental shops will come to your accommodation to kit you out - far preferable to wait in the comfort of your own chalet rather than the stuffy and stressful surrounds of a equipment shop. In the shops Saturday afternoons and Sunday mornings are still the busiest time to get equipment. All of the satellite villages and the suburbs have at least 1 rental shop (of varying quality) so you don't have to go to Méribel Centre - though the choice there is more extensive.

handy to know

Getting the **right equipment** will ensure you fully enjoy your holiday. Your feet will hurt if you don't get well-fitting boots so don't be embarrassed to persevere until you find a pair that fits. If they cause you problems on the slopes take them back - all the shops will help you find a more suitable pair. Unless you know you want a specific type or make of ski, take the advice of the ski fitter. They are the experts and will know which is the best ski for you based on your ability and age. One reason to go to a particular shop is if your hotel or tour operator has arranged a rental deal with them - you may get a cheaper rate or insurance thrown in for free, so it's worth checking. Most shops stock a varied range of the latest ski equipment from all the usual manufacturers - Salomon, Atomic, Rossignol and Dynastar - but you will have to search a little harder if you're looking for Völkl or Fischer. And because there are so many places to hire equipment, prices are competitive. Equipment for children is often available at a reduced rate - price is normally worked out on the basis of height rather than age. At most shops you can take out **insurance** (except on test skis) to cover accidental breakage, loss or theft - though skiing on roads is not insurable. Unfortunately skis do get stolen or taken by accident - with so many people skiing on similar skis it's easy for confusion to arise. When you stop for lunch or après it's a good idea to swap one of your skis with a friend so you both have a mis-matched pair. This helps to ensure that nobody will pick up your skis, either by mistake or otherwise.

for skis

freeride (t 0479 005221) is the leader of the new wave. On its website (i freeride.fr), you can reserve rental skis and boots before your arrival, guaranteeing you the equipment you want and saving time. One of the first to offer a fitting service in your accommodation they also collect the equipment at the end of your stay. For those in the market to buy, the test centre is excellent - you can try any number of skis from their range (of Salomons, K2s or Heads) for a maximum of 2 hours before finally choosing - not one for the indecisive. Their shop, should you need to visit, is in the Centre's Tremplin complex and has ranges of Patagonia clothing.

If you know you want Salomon skis or boots, then the **snowrider** shop on the upper level of the Galerie des Cimes is the place to head, where you will find a helpful Scotsman.

intersport also offers online equipment reservation (i meribelskirental.com) and will collect you by minibus and collect your equipment at the end of your holiday.

In Mottaret, all of the shops are similar from the equipment they rent to the prices they charge, and all are part of ski rental chains.

for boots

freeride is also the choice for boots - their staff attend an intensive training session beofre the season starts. And if you want to buy, in-soles are made to measure - so they should be as comfortable as ski boots get.

georges manduit in the Galerie des Gentianes in Méribel Centre (just above the tourist office) fits boots using the Conform'able system.

for boards

Méribel has 2 specialist boarding shops. **board brains** is the English choice - run by an affable Englishman, the selection of boards (including Santa Cruz, Burton and Nitro) and bindings (including Flow) to rent or buy is extensive, despite the small size of the shop. The range of accessories and clothing is as impressive. And if your board has got too friendly with too many rocks they will give you an honest apprasial of its salvagability and rescue it if possible.

oxygène in the Tremplin complex in Méribel Centre is Board Brains' main competitor. French-run, it is open over the lunch-time siesta. Flow bindings are also available.

for other equipment

Rental shops offer a lot more than just skis and boards. Most stock a wide range of ski clothing - although brands differ from shop to shop so you will need to shop around if you are looking for a specific make - and all the accessories you can think of. There is little difference from what you would pay for the same clothes in the UK. Most places will hire telemarks, snowblades, avalanche transceivers and snowshoes. For touring skis, you have to search a bit harder, though Intersport in the Galerie des Cimes will provide you with everything that you need for a tour. Sport 2000 in the Tremplin complex is the only place from which you can hire snowskates.

As with many French resorts, the biggest presence in Méribel is exerted by the ESF (Ecole de Ski Français). Though there are more red jackets than pistes that's not to say that it's your only choice. A number of smaller ski schools have also been established - these tend to be more specialised and you can be more sure about who will be teaching you. In fact some of them are so small you may find that you are being taught by the boss. With over 500 instructors in the whole valley, even if he's not available you should be able to find somebody to teach you.

handy to know

group lessons are the cheapest way to learn to ski. When you book you will be asked your level of skiing/boarding ability, either by the colour of piste you are comfortable on, the number of weeks you have skied before, or by the vague 'beginner/intermediate/advanced' pigeonholes. In practice the divisions aren't as accurate as they could be - some people overestimate their ability or misunderstand words like 'confident' and 'controlled', so to and extent the level of your group is pot luck. If you are honest about your skill level you are likely to find yourself (vaguely) in the right place.

If you have the money, **private lessons** are without question the way forward. Once you're past the basics, individual attention is the best way to significantly improve your technique and is often better value. If you can get a group of four or more the individual price per day is similar to the average price per day for group lessons, with the advantage that you go where you want to go and practise what you want to practise. The length of private lessons varies from school to school, but generally the divisions are simply for a half day (morning or afternoon) or a full day. A half day will be 3 hours of instruction on one side of lunch.

prices are pretty standard across the board - though you may pay a little more for the smaller companies, there's not much in it. If you book group lessons you can have a week's worth of half-day instruction for only a little more than it costs to rent your skis. Private lessons (and guides) are a different story, but again you won't find too much variation in what the different schools charge.

Though there are no specialist **boarding** schools in Méribel and Mottaret, most of the schools offer surf lessons, though private lessons may be your only option. The skill divisions, prices, times and overall format is much the same as with skiing.

Either make your **booking** before you get to Méribel - by email, fax or phone - or once you're in resort, in person at the ski school office. Always pre-book in peak season, as there are not enough instructors to meet demand - schools recommend booking at least 2 weeks in advance and in peak weeks more time in advance to ensure you get your first option. To confirm your booking, the schools will need your name, level of ability and a credit card number.

The main **meeting points** are found at La Chaudanne in Méribel Centre and on the *Front de Neige* (Snow Front) in Mottaret. There is also an ESF meeting point at the Rond-Point. The rest of the suburbs and satellite villages do not have any meeting points - so if you're taking lessons you'll have to do a bit of travelling first.

It is illegal to teach in France without a qualification recognised by the French establishment. In effect this means that the majority of **instructors** in France are French, as few other 'international' qualifications are accepted and the equivalence race test that foreign instructors must pass is extremely difficult. But this approach gives you the advantage of knowing that your instructor is at the least a very competent skier or boarder.

Almost all instructors speak good **english** and there are also instructors who speak every other language - though you will need to book a long way in advance should you want instruction in a language less common to the Alps.

Lessons take place **whatever the weather**, unless the entire lift system is closed in which case the school will refund the full lesson price. They will also refund you if you are ill or have an accident and can produce a valid medical certificate. If you cancel a lesson for any other reason, your chances of getting a refund are relative to how much notice you give the school, and how charming you are when you cancel.

esf

0479 086031
0479 086080
@ esfmeribel@wanadoo.fr
W3 esf-meribel.com
tourist office (méribel & mottaret)

As with the ESF in other French resorts, whether you have a good or bad experience will depend upon whether you have a good or bad instructor - and simply thanks to the law of averages among the 450 instructors in the Méribel valley some of them are fantastic and some of them aren't. Instructors are generally allocated sensibly - if you book a private lesson for your kids they will try to choose someone that's good with kids and can speak reasonable English - but the demand during peak season is such that you basically get what you get, in a sort of lucky dip fashion. The valley has 4 ESF offices - 1 in the tourist office in the Centre, 1 at La Chaudanne (t 0479 085881), 1 at Le Rond-Point (t 0479 088942) and 1 in Mottaret (t 0479 0049 49). One of the best options for adults offered by the Méribel school is the "3 Valleys - Blue" and the "3 Valleys - Red" afternoon tours - 2 alternatives determined by ability level. The "Ski Discovery" days offers skiers the opportunity to discover the lesser known parts of the 3 Vallees without having to employ the services of a guide. The school also run a programme of snowshoeing and cross-country ski activities.

magic in motion

0479 085336
0479 003140
@ meribel@magicinmotion.co.uk
W3 magicinmotion.co.uk
galerie des cimes

The boys from Magic in Motion are hard to miss - their ski suits are an alarming and somewhat lurid combination of purple and orange. But don't let this put you off. Though they have schools in other resorts, Méribel is their flagship. The school offers the usual array of group and private lessons, as well as options such as "couloirs and extreme" and "steep and deep" - no explanation required for either. Their lessons for children also have a good reputation. And at least you'll be able to see them should the weather close in.

ski academy

0479 081199
0479 083939
@ meribel@ski-academy.com
W3 ski-academy.com
sport 2000

Ski Academy's main branch is in Courchevel 1850, but the school has recently based a handful of instructors in Méribel, operating out of Sport 2000 in the Tremplin Complex. A French owned ski school with an English focus, most of the instructors are English. Group lessons take a maximum of 8, meaning you'll certainly get more attention than with the ESF. New for 2004 are the semi-private lessons during low season - for adults and children in groups of 3-5. In addition, Ski Academy run children's lessons outside of the school holidays - most of the other schools don't. They don't run group snowboarding lessons, but boarders (and skiers) can join one of the snowsports clinics - a more intensive course over 2½ days of tuition with video feedback.

new generation

0479 010318
0479 081199
@ info@skinewgen.com
W3 skinewgen.com
freeride

New Generation or "NewGen" is another of the British offerings. Established 6 years ago its main office is in Courchevel 1650 operating out of the English-run Freeride shop. They have the same location in Méribel - all of its instructors speak English and most are BASI qualified and though some are French if you book a group lesson they will guarantee that your instructor is English. They operate the usual programme of lessons, but come into their own with their ski performance clinics. In addition they can provide coaching for off-piste technique and ISIA qualifications.

and the rest

There is a lengthy list of very small ski schools. In additions to lessons **absolute ski** (t 0479 550983, i absolute-ski.com) will also organise off-piste and heli-skiing. **euro ski adventures** (t 0479 007433, i euroskiadventure.com) is a French school who run introduction to powder lessons as well as the usual courses. All of the instructors at **parallel lines** (t 0479 003221, i parallel-lines.com) are English and BASI qualified. **snow glisse** (t 0607 771225, i snowglisse.com) runs private lessons only but for both skiers and snowboarders. The sweetly named **snowd'light** (t 0664 118883, i snowdlight.com) also only offers private tuition and focusses on tailor-made programmes to give you as much flexibility as possible. **snow systems** (t 0479 004022/0607 155022, i snow-systems.com) promises "quality not quantity" - it has meeting points at La Chaudanne and in Mottaret. **ski principle** (t 0479 005271) is a husband and wife team who are known for getting results with nervous skiers.

By far the best - and safest - way to make the most of the off-piste is to hire a qualified mountain guide. As they have spent years getting to know and understand the mountain terrain, not only will they find the best powder but you can trust them to look after your security.

The difference between **guides and instructors** is fundamental - instructing is about 'how' and guiding is about 'where'. Ski instructors are not permitted to take you off-piste and you should not ask them to. In contrast the limiting factor with a guide is your own ability. If you are competent enough they will take you anywhere you want to go. There is no question of a guide's ability. Becoming one takes years and requires an intimate knowledge of everything the mountains have to offer particularly how to be safe in this notoriously unpredictable environment. Guides are not just expert skiers, first and foremost they are mountaineers: physically fit individuals, with extensive experience of mountain rescue, practice and procedure. They are also proficient rock and ice climbers and are competent and comfortable in all types of conditions. During the course of qualifying, they are tested on alpine technique, avalanche rescue and first aid, to name but a few. The very definition of a safe pair of hands.

Méribel's Bureau des Guides (t 0479 003038) is based in the Parc Olympic at La Chaudanne with a manned desk 5pm-7pm. The range of activities on offer is extensive - off-piste skiing, glacier skiing, ski touring and heliskiing in Italy. They will also show you around the pistes - but don't expect them to be too excited about doing it. From time to the Bureau holds free demonstrations of how to use mountain safety equipment, such as avalanche transceivers. An alternative is the ski school **ski sensations** (t 0608 741829, i ski-sensations.com), which specialises in tailor-made programmes, and though they run on piste group and private lessons their strength is in off-piste tuition and guiding.

If you decide to hire a guide, don't underestimate how fit you need to be to get the most out of the experience. Whilst the guide will cater the day to the standard of the least able skier in the group, he may still lead you along some tiring traverses or climbs to reach the best snow.

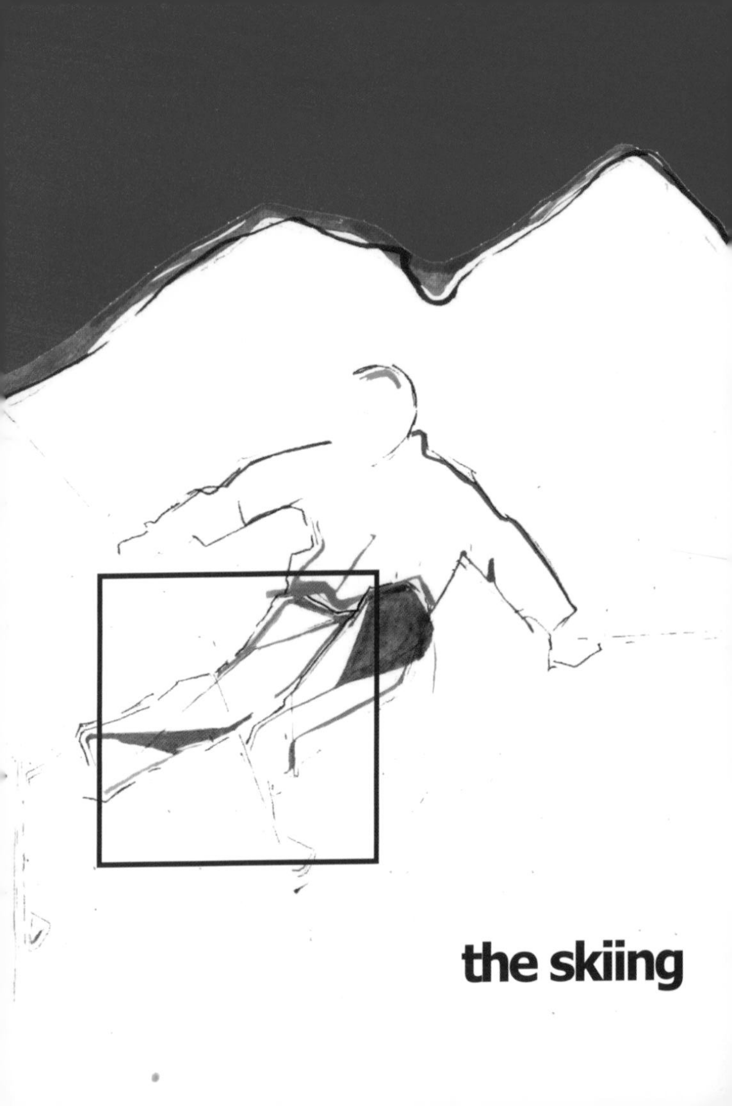
the skiing

The Méribel valley lies between the Saint Bon valley (home to the Courchevel resorts) and the Belleville valley (home to St. Martin de Belleville, Les Menuires and Val Thorens), delineated by 2 ridge lines - the rough jagged peaks of Saulire on the east side towards Courchevel and the smoother Tougnète on the west side to Belleville. It has the lowest overall altitude of the 3 valleys, but being at the heart of the area all the skiing is within easy reach so you never feel too far from home. The slopes in the Méribel valley face east, west and north - so in good weather, some part of the valley will be in the sunshine. The downside of this is that the snow tends to disappear more quickly than elsewhere, especially at village level. The lower altitude and exposure to the sun gives the piste bashers and snow cannons a harder job to maintain the snow than in the Courchevel or Belleville valleys, but a fleet of the former and hundreds (500) of the latter work hard to perfect the slopes. A lot of skiers disregard the skiing in this valley, thinking of it as little more than the way to get between Val Thorens and Courchevel - but this does not do it justice. There is a great variety of pistes, with some wonderfully long descents - and because so many skiers are in a great hurry to get elsewhere much of the area can be enjoyed in relative quietness. The vast numbers of skiers moving through the valley from Courchevel to Val Thorens and vice versa can be detrimental to the snow conditions and cause bottlenecks, paricularly in Mottaret, but if you know where to go the skiing is some of the best in all the 3 Vallées.

snapshot

méribel
132kms of pistes - 11 green, 33 blue, 21 red, 9 black
53 lifts - 16 gondolas, 17 chairlifts, 20 draglifts
off-piste - 28kms of itinerary routes, some tree-skiing & couloirs
highest point 2952m
2 snowparks

3 vallées
600kms pistes - 68 green, 104 blue, 110 red, 35 black
189 lifts - 36 gondolas, 68 chairlifts, 80 draglifts, 2 cable cars, 3 funitels
off-piste - something for everyone: couloirs, trees, powder bowls
highest point 3200m
10 snowparks

pistes

On the mountain, there is a menagerie of pistes, including biche (deer), geai (jay), and cerf (stag) and a proliferation of runs called marmotte. They are signposted reasonably well and also numbered (though the numbers do not appear on the official piste map). Links between the different valleys are displayed on yellow boards - confusing for those used to itinerary routes being marked in yellow. The piste system adopts the same colour-coding used in all European resorts (➥ 'pistes' in the glossary) but this should only be used as a general guide. Although the gradient or width of each individual piste stays the same, other features such as snow conditions can change daily. A blue piste can become more testing than a nearby red, because it is over-crowded with skiers of ranging abilities or because of poor or icy conditions. And personal feelings about pistes vary greatly - an easy blue to one skier can seem like a vertical drop to another. The limits of the pistes are marked by poles - so you can orientate yourself and at least know when you are on a piste. The pole on the left edge is the colour of the piste - green, blue, red or black - whilst the pole defining the right edge of each piste is similarly coloured, with a small band of bright orange at the top.

off-piste

The resort does not include itinerary routes on its official piste map, and so our descriptions of the 'off-piste' include any routes, recognised or otherwise that are not groomed or checked at the end of the day. If you intend to venture away from the markers it is best to do so in the company of a mountain guide. As you would expect within such a huge ski area, you will find plenty of ungroomed snow alongside and in between pistes on which to practise your technique without going too far.

lifts

Like the pistes, the lifts are named (on the mountain and on the official piste map). On the whole the quality and quantity of lifts is good, with a total capacity of 240,000 skiers per hour. Only a few bottlenecks exist, primarily at the main ascending points for the resorts, and where the lifts deal with skiers crossing from 1 valley to another. Though the queuing system has some way to go to compare to the American or Canadian resorts, it is better organised than some. The ski schools often have a priority queue and some lifts have a quick queue for single skiers and/or families. At some lifts, children under a certain height must be accompanied. That the lifts in the Méribel valley are maintained by 2 lift companies is significant only for lift pass purposes (➥ lift passes). Most of the lifts open in early December - and the remainder by Christmas - and run until the middle or end of April. The exact date changes yearly and if the snow conditions are good, the lifts may open earlier or close later than advertised. In late February, March and April the lifts generally open half an hour earlier and close half an hour later than in the first half of the season. The lifts in the 3 Vallées are open for a longer day than in many other resorts, giving you the longest skiing day - in the second half of the season, some lifts don't close until 5pm. Opening and closing times are noted at the bottom of each lift and on the official piste map.

Wherever you ski, it is a good idea to work out which will be the last lift you will take to return home and check what time it closes.

the areas

The 3 Vallées is divided into 11 sectors for the purpose of the maps in this guide - these are arranged in sequence on the overview map (➡ inside back cover flap) from the Courchevel valley in the east to the Belleville valley in the west. The Courchevel valley is divided into 3 sectors (a-c), as is the Méribel valley (d-f) while the Belleville valley is divided into 5 sectors (g-k). In this chapter you'll find a description of how to get to and from the slopes, the general characteristics and aspect of the area, and detail of the pistes, the off-piste, the mountain restaurants and the local après for each area. The Méribel valley is described first, then the Courchevel valley and finally the Belleville valley:

méribel
saulire (map d)
tougnète (map e)
mont du vallon (map f)
courchevel
courchevel 1850 (map b)
courchevel 1650 (map a)
la tania, le praz & 1550 (map c)
belleville
st. martin (map g)
les menuires (map h)
le masse (map i)
val thorens & maurienne (map j & k)

At the back of the book there is a more detailed table of lift information and a ski map for each area (in which the piste colours correspond to those used by the resort).

coming & going

Where you start depends a little upon where you staying. The lifts at La Chaudanne give you the most option - taking you up both the Saulire and the Tougnète sides. La Chaudanne is the starting point for those staying in **méribel centre** and where you will find the main lift pass office, WCs, ski lockers, an information hut and a large underground pay & display car park. A quieter (and free) parking area can be found along the road towards Mottaret - and access gained from there to the Chaudanne lifts by a short ski down the piste running parallel to the road.

You can get to La Chaudanne from any of the suburbs or the satellite villages by bus - though timing operates a bit of French laissez-faire. The buses are also inadequately sized to deal with the number of people wanting to use them. In the suburbs of **le rond-point** and **belvédère** much of the accommodation lies close to the piste so you can also ski down to La Chaudanne quite easily. From **l'altiport** there is a choice of 2 lifts - which take you about mid-way up the Saulire side of Méribel. If you are staying in Méribel Centre, Le Rond-Point or L'Altiport, as long as you finish your skiing day on the Saulire side of the mountain, you should be able to ski as close to your door as possible - the blue piste (Doron) runs alongside the edge of these areas. The same is true for Belvédère, though the red piste (Manduit) brings you closer.

morel has its own chairlift (Morel) that takes you to L'Altiport on the Saulire side of the mountain, making access to the Courchevel valley easy. Alternatively you can ski the piste (after a short walk to reach it) down to La Chaudanne. It is not possible to return by lift to Morel or 1600, but you can ski back for most of the season.

méribel village also has its own lift (the Golf chair) that links to the skiing at L'Altiport - handy if you want to ski on the Saulire side or get to the Courchevel valley. It's not possible to return to Méribel Village by lift, but the piste bashers work hard to ensure that you can always return on skis. On the rare occasion you can't, the only option is a bus ride from wherever you finish your skiing day.

The Olympe gondola from Brides-les-Bains to Méribel stops in the lower villages of **les allues** and **le raffort** and ends next to the Parc Olympique at La Chaudanne. You can ski back to Les Allues and Le Raffort along a piste from the Tougnète side of the valley - though this needs good snow conditions to be passable. The quickest way to get home is back down on the Olympe gondola - though the bus is also an option.

If you can't ski in or out from where you are staying in **mottaret** you need to find a new travel agent. Most of the accommodation is next to or within a short walking distance of one of the pistes that lead to the hub of lifts at the bottom of the resort. The same pistes that take you to the lifts in the morning bring you home at the end of the day.

In the descriptions for the ski areas 'access' is explained from La Chaudanne in Méribel and the resort centre in Mottaret.

beginners

It is difficult to imagine a more ideal place to learn than the 3 Vallées - though Val d'Isère would argue for joint first place. Each of the 3 Vallées resort has a designated nursery slope area and in Méribel the lifts running alongside the nursery slopes are free. A word of warning though, if you put on skis for the first time in the 3 Vallées, anywhere else may disappoint - the skiing is easy to access and you can often ski to the door at the end of the day. That said if you are only just starting out, there is enough in the 3 Vallées to keep you busy for a number of years.

In Méribel the Altiport area was developed with beginners in mind. It helps that the slopes run over the gently undulating surface of a (snow-covered) golf course. Not only can you buy a lift pass just for the lifts in this area (➥ lift passes), but there is a proliferation of wide and well-groomed green and blue pistes ideal for nervous novices. An easy chairlift and a gentle button lift make for good practice. And as the Altiport lies at the one end of the Saulire area, it is not used as a thoroughfare by other skiers.

Skiers who are 1 turn above absolute beginner should consider buying a 3 Vallées lift pass as there are easy runs in both of the other valleys.

Mottaret is not so ideal. Though the blue runs just above the resort are easily accessible they suffer from poorer conditions than elsewhere - in part because of the sheer volume of skiing traffic. The runs themselves are on the top edge of the blue band and may be daunting to absolute beginners. These runs are used by more experienced skiers and boarders returning from the skiing in the Belleville valley and Mont du Vallon who may not have the patience to dodge beginners.

intermediates

It is also arguable that there is no better ski area for intermediates - with a seemingly never-ending network of well-groomed runs. Even those with a real mission to ski the whole area are unlikely to do so in a week. If the lift system is fully functional, you won't run out of things to ski. Pick any point on the mountain and you can choose between blue, red or black depending upon how up for it you, and your legs, are feeling or how much wine you indulged in the night before.

experts

While the 3 Vallées is rarely talked about in the same hallowed terms as Chamonix, experts skiers will find some runs of interest. When all links are open the world is your oyster, and if you know where to look there is plenty of steep and scary. In Méribel the Face (the site of the 1992 Olympic ladies downhill) is always fun while over in Courchevel the infamous Couloirs may send some scuttling back to the nearby reds. If strong winds or unfriendly conditions keep the higher lifts closed, you may feel frustrated. Except for 1 black piste (from the 1st station of the Tougnète gondola), the lower slopes around Méribel and Mottaret are mainly green and blue - so if you can't get high, you won't get steep. Even when it's all systems go, the motorway feel of many of the pistes (particularly in the over-groomed environs of Courchevel) may not excite. To explore the lesser known off-piste the best advice is to hire a guide - none of the itinerary maps are marked on the official piste map.

boarders

As long as you avoid the pancake flat Ours and Truite pistes, you can't go too wrong. There is the occasional schuss/narrow path to keep you focussed. On the flipside, most of the main links are by chairlift or gondola, and even where there is a button lift, there is also normally an alternative for the poma-phobic. And you won't find a t-bar in the whole ski area.

The Méribel valley also rewards boarders with 2 snowparks - the Moonpark de L'Arpasson above Méribel and the Plattières snowpark above Mottaret. They win plaudits for their composition and good maintenance (including the half-pipes). The Moonpark is generally regarded as the better of the two and you can get a lift pass that allows you to use it for 3 days of your choice during the season. Elsewhere there are 4 parks in the Courchevel valley and 4 in the Belleville valley.

non-skiers

As a non-skier, the main reason to go up the mountain is to admire the views. The 3 Vallées is very much about skiing and does not cater so well for those reluctant to strap planks to their feet. The designated footpaths are on the flatter pistes or away from them altogether so you don't have to worry too much about being knocked over by an out-of-control skier. With a pedestrian lift pass (➥ lift passes) you can go up in any of the gondolas or cable cars, but not the chairs or button lifts for obvious reasons. There are numerous walking trails within the valley from strolls through the villages and forests to half-day hikes. The trails are marked and regularly groomed, but they are not supervised - further information about where they are can be obtained from the tourist office.

The jagged teeth of the Saulire peaks give the eastern side of the Méribel valley an impressive skyline. At 2738m it is higher than the opposite (Tougnète) side and from the top the eye is treated to a sea of peaks in the Belleville valley and far, far beyond. If you want to spend the afternoon skiing in the sun, head over to this side of the valley - as the slopes face west, the final rays of the day fall here, also making it the better side for sun-baked après. Later on in the season the snow doesn't get the brunt of the sun until the second half of the day. From the top of Saulire there are any number of vertical choices - reds running in parallel to blues interspersed with a few friendly greens and the occasional less friendly black - and the upper slopes are rarely overcrowded. It's difficult to pick a favourite or the best - they all go the same way and on a similar gradient, but if it makes you happy to be on a blue, then there are plenty to choose from. And if you're looking for vertical descents you will find them here - over 1000m from the top of Saulire to Mottaret and another 300m on top of that from the top to La Chaudanne in the centre of Méribel.

access

The Burgin gondola from La Chaudanne takes you to the top of Saulire (stopping at a mid-station lower down) - easy if you are staying in the very centre of Méribel and can walk to La Chaudanne.

map d

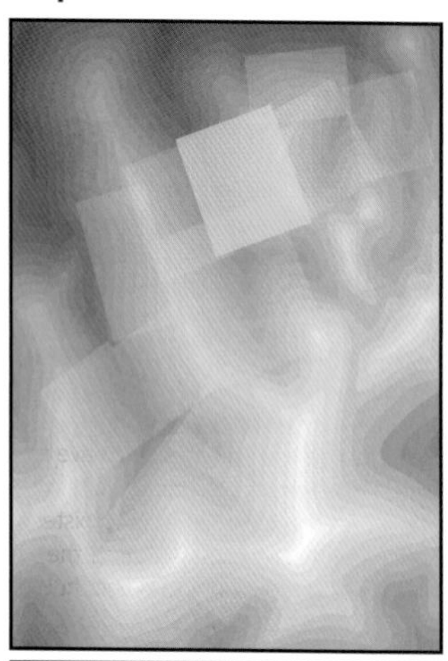

snapshot

out of interest
highest point - 2738m
aspect - w
pistes - beginner-friendly greens, wide and gentle blues, long and fun red & noir blacks
off-piste - the valley's steepest couloir
restaurants - 7

highlights & hotspots
tree-hugging at the altiport
1300m of vertical descent
après at le rond-point
sunny afternoons
use of your 3 vallées ski pass

From elsewhere, you'll probably have to don skis first, or catch a bus. The Rhodos gondola takes you to the pistes above the Altiport. From Mottaret, the Pas du Lac gondola from the main hub of lifts at the bottom of the resort (a short ski from most of Mottaret's accommodation) also takes you to the top of Saulire - though again you can get off at a mid-station.

pistes

The best of the valley's **green** pistes are found just above the Altiport. Wide and prettily lined with trees they are very friendly to newcomers to skiing.

The highest **blue** starts from the Col de la Loze plateau and can only be described as boring - a long flat path, it is nothing more than one of the ways to get home from the skiing in nearby Courchevel. The rest of the blues are much more fun - confidence boosting for beginners and speedy for anybody else.

The long **red** (Pic Noir) at the northern end of the valley is one of the most fun runs in the 3 Vallées. Though it is not always open at the beginning of the season (because of inadequate snow coverage), when it is it's a fabulous sweeping descent through the forest to the pistes above the Altiport. At the end you need some speed to avoid an anti-climatic pole. The longest red (Manduit) runs from the top of Saulire to La Chaudanne, the full length of the mountain, though the very top is a bit hairy - the steeper gradient turns skiers into mogul creators, not helped by a large rock in the middle of the piste. If you can't avoid the other skiers, you should definitely avoid this at the very least.

There are 3 **black** runs, all of which deserve their grading because of their unpredictable conditions. Tetras from the Col de la Loze is often mogulled and patchy. The Grande Rosière, at the other end of the valley, doesn't get the sun until the afternoon, and often resembles a skating rink for most of the day, as does the Sanglier.

off-piste

Though there are no **itinerary routes** on the official piste map, one of the best known ones runs through Méribel Village to Brides-les-Bains. Passing through fields and forests, and involving a lot of tree dodging, it is only open if there has been exceptional snowfall - only worth the effort so you can say you've done it. Otherwise the Saulire peak offers one of the most serious **off-piste** descents in the valley - the narrow and rocky couloir visible from the Burgin gondola as you ascend to the top. Even steeper than its Courchevel cousins, as it is south facing it is also prone to less favourable conditions especially by the afternoon when the sun has done its damage. Those with more sense than skill will find plenty of ungroomed snow in between the pistes for a taster of the fluffy stuff and some fun can be had tree-dodging through the forest at the Altiport.

eating & drinking

Eating on the mountain isn't one of the highlights of the Méribel valley - the options are pretty samey and pretty pricey. Eating in the resort is always an option - there are numerous places near La Chaudanne, good hotel restaurants at Le Rond-Point and the Altiport as well as Le Lodge du Village in Méribel Village. In Mottaret, the area around the resort's main hub of lifts turns into a mass picnic site, as many of the slope-side eateries are take-away. Of them the best is the serving hatch at the side of Mottaret's small supermarket, where you can get chicken and chips and hot sandwiches.

le rond-point (t 0479 003751) is a one-stop shop for morning coffee, lunch, and après. Ideal for mixed ability groups - it can reached by green, blue and red pistes - non-skiers can also join in the fun as it also just above the Rond-Point bus stop. Ably run by a predominantly English team, the menu is "international", offering something different from the usual regional specialities - such as wok-fried beef. In clement weather lunch is served on a large terrace. When it is bad, everything moves inside and also upstairs to a charming wooden room under the eaves. For a quick lunch, the snack bar (the Petit Rond-Point) below the main restaurant serves sandwiches and other snacks at reasonable prices (and you can check your emails). Reservations for the à la carte restaurant are essential.

The **adray télébar** hotel (t 0479 086026) on the edge of the Doron piste just below Le Rond-Point is a pleasant spot for lunch, with a lovely south-facing terrace.

At the top of the Altiport button lift, **les rhododendrons** (t 0479 005092) is a large 2 level restaurant with self- and table-service options. With its location at the top of Méribel's nursery slope area, the self-service is often over-crowded with families battling for spaghetti bolognaise before the afternoon lessons begin.

le chardonnet (t 0479 004481) is lovely inside and out and with its wooden beams and stone walls is top of the class for adhering strictly to the Méribel architectural rules. The food is pleasant but suffers from typically French and very slow service.

Slightly lower down the hill is **le choucas** (t 0479 005831). Built in 1962 this was the first mountain restaurant in the valley. Situated at the Burgin gondola mid-station, if you're looking for a late breakfast, try the "oeufs choucas".

At the top of the Pas du Lac 2 gondola, **les pierres plates** (t 0479 004641) is the highest restaurant on Saulire and the best thing about it is the view over to Mont du Vallon and beyond. Because of its location it is a great place to catch the last of the sunshine before an alcohol injected ski home, but beware the strength of the *rhum chocolat*.

côte 2000 (t 0479 005540) is the last slope-side stop on the descent down from Saulire to Mottaret. It is also open in the evening (if there are enough reservations) for those who fancy a fondue on the mountain.

If you object to spending £20 for a croque-monsieur and a coke, a **picnic** is an alternative. And as there are benches at the top of the Col de la Loze plateau, by the Burgin gondola mid-station and at various points on the forest around the Altiport it is a fairly civilised option.

For après the **rond-point** with its live music is the obvious choice - the only place on this side of the mountain where you find live bands - not least because it's only a short ski home. If it gets too blurry to connect boot to binding, the bus-stop is nearby. A more civilised alternative is just up the hill - in the **yéti** hotel, with its delightful terrace overlooking the pistes.

getting home

From the Saulire side you can reach the main resort, the suburbs and Méribel Village on skis. The blue (Doron) option is the overcrowded endpoint for all runs down from the Altiport, but has exits along the way for Le Rond-Point and the rest of the accommodation in the suburbs. Better skiers should opt for the Manduit red - it is often completely deserted and passes by Bélvèdere on its way down to the village. The way home to Mottaret is blue - though by the end of it that's what less confident skiers may feel.
If you'd rather rest your legs, you can get back to Méribel by lift - the Burgin-Saulire gondola takes you back to La Chaudanne. The Rhodos also takes you there, from its top station above the Altiport or from its mid-station by Le Rond-Point. To get to Mottaret catch the Pas du Lac gondola, either from the top of Saulire or half way down.

Méribel's Tougnète side wakes up in the sun (on good weather days) so if you like to avoid the morning ice, this is your best bet. The ridge is the divide between Méribel and the Belleville valley and the skiing above the resorts of Les Menuires and Saint Martin de Belleville.

access

As for the Saulire side, the main lifts up to the Tougnète skiing start at La Chaudanne - reached by the lucky few on foot, but for the majority on skis or by bus. Once at La Chaudanne, there are 3 ways to get up the mountain - so take your pick depending upon weather and queues. The most direct route to the very top is on the Tougnète gondola, which ends at the top of the ridge. To get there from Mottaret you can ski down the Truite green to La Chaudanne or take your chances on the Combes and then the Table Verte chairlifts.

pistes

The only **green** is the Truite, which links Méribel to Mottaret - and is often festooned with beginners.

There are loads of **blues** - though all are much of a muchness in terms of gradient and nature but provide ideal practise for beginners.

The **reds** are even fewer but fun - all follow a similar line down the mountain from the top of the Tougnète ridge.

map e

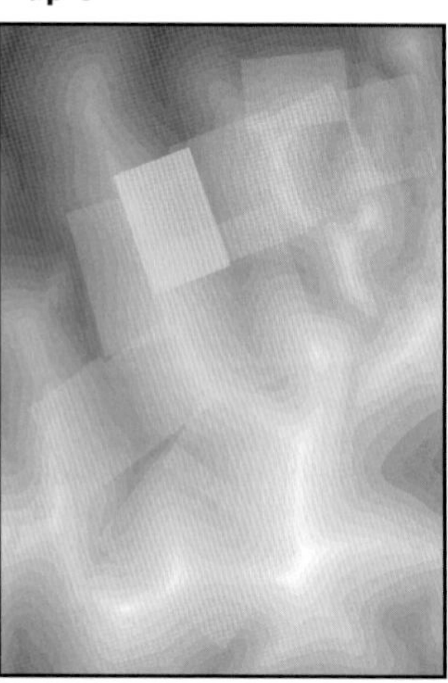

snapshot

out of interest
highest point - 2434m
aspect - e
pistes - a very flat green, plentiful blues, plentiful reds & the resort's most famous black
off-piste - itinerary route to les allues
restaurants - 3

highlights & hotspots
the olympic (face) black
the moonpark
can be cold in the afternoon in early winter
easily accessed off-piste

One of the enduring remains of the 1992 Winter Olympics is the Face **black** run. Conditions are variable - not only daily but at different points on the run itself. The black called Les Bosses ('bosses' is French for moguls) lives up to its name. Higher up, Combe Tougnète starts off steep, though it looks worse from the approach lift (the Tougnète 2 gondola) than it actually is.

snowpark

One of the 2 snowparks in the valley, and regarded as the best, at the Moonpark de L'Arpasson you will find 2 half-pipes (1 competition standard and 1 for those not quite so good), a number of graded jumps and a 1km boardercross. It's less busy than the snowpark above Mottaret (➥ Mont du Vallon) so it's the perfect place to try out your tricks in (relative) private.

off-piste

An **itinerary route** runs from the top of Roc de Fer down to Le Raffort and ultimately the village of Les Allues. It is only skiable after a lengthy dump of snow, but is neither particularly difficult nor easy.

eating & drinking

As for the Saulire side of the mountain you can ski down to the centre of Méribel for lunch. One option is **les castors** (t 0479 085279) a long-standing and local-run restaurant at the foot of the green (Truite) piste. Sit down meals and take-away are possible.

les crêtes (t 0479 085650/0609 405104) is a low-slung, cosy little restaurant on the top of the Tougnète ridge. Cuisine is traditional and the restaurant is known for its Tartiflette (a potato-based dish) - one of the best ways to warm up the extremities. On sunny days the views from the terrace are awesome - although as the restaurant terrace has a fairly exposed aspect it is rarely enjoyable.

arpasson (t 0479 004348) near stage 1 of the Tougnète gondola offers both table and self-service. The terrace is pleasant for an afternoon vin chaud as you return down the mountain.

For official **picnics** take your sandwiches to the benches at the top of the Caves lift. For something more spontaneous just pick a patch of snow.

getting home

Those staying in Les Allues or Raffort should relish the opportunity to get home on skis - along the Villages blue run, when conditions are good. To Centre the choice is an easy (though often slushy) blue or a more tricky (and often bumpy) black. For Mottaret, the blue run which starts just below the Tougnète mid-station runs alongside the edge of Laitelet's accommodation. The only way to get down to Méribel by lift is on the Tougnète gondola, which you can join at the top or the mid-station.

If you had to describe the skiing on Mont du Vallon in 1 word it would be 'long'. Lovely, lengthy lines unfold from the peak - though this guide uses the name to describe the skiing in the surrounding area as well. From Mont du Vallon to the bottom of the Mûres Rouges chairlift is around 1100m and from the top of the Plattières gondola it is 1000m to Mottaret. The north facing aspect keeps the snow light and powdery but because of the altitude (2952m at the top), the area is sensitive to inclement weather - if bad weather hits, it hits here first. Mont du Vallon closes at the first rumour of a breeze, as does the Côte Brune chairlift, and with it any chance of getting to Val Thorens. One side of the Mont du Vallon peak is home to the beautiful Reserve Naturelle de Tueda, a national park in which no skiing is permitted - if you do venture in and are caught you can be heavily fined. The only drawback to the area is that the runs are used by skiers staying in the Courchevel and Méribel valleys to get to the skiing around the resort of Val Thorens - and then at the end of the day to get home so they can be very busy.

access

The easiest way to reach the Mont du Vallon peak itself is by taking the Plattières gondola out of Mottaret to its second stage, then ski down the red or blue Bouvreuil (chaffinch) run to the Mont du Vallon gondola. Skiers staying

map f

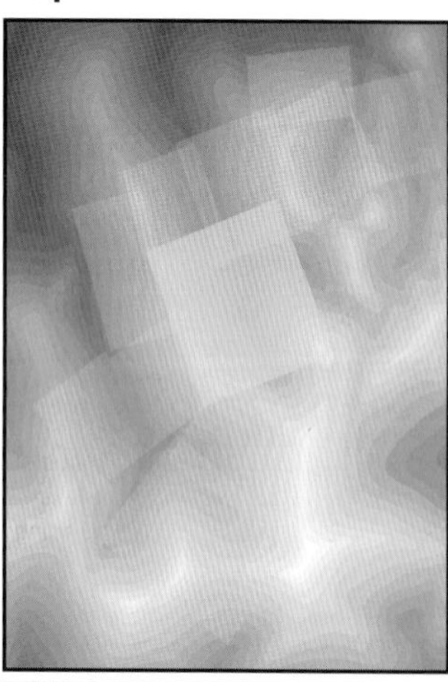

snapshot

out of interest
highest point - 2952m
aspect - n, e
pistes - a range of very flat to fairly steep blues, lengthy reds & a lone black
off-piste - numerous itinerary routes & shortcuts between pistes
restaurants - 3

highlights & hotspots
lovely, long descents
bottlenecks at the plan des mains chairlift
vulnerable to bad weather
light and powdery snow

in Méribel can get to Mottaret by bus or by taking the Burgin gondola from La Chaudanne to its mid-station and skiing down to Mottaret.

pistes

green is not a colour that appears on this part of the piste map and so **blue** is as easy as it gets and the range in difficulty is extensive. Both boarders and skiers should beware the frustratingly flat track (Ours) - though this has been improved for the 2004 season - through the forest from the bottom of the Mûres Rouges chairlift to Mottaret. Its pancake tendancies have been the flatfall (rather than downfall) of many a man.

red alert - they are numerous in this area. The highlight is the duo from the top of the Mont du Vallon peak. The 5kms Combe du Vallon run is the longer of the two - but be aware you need to take the Mûres Rouges chairlift back up or face the blue Ours run - but neither suffers for lack of vertical descent.

The Bartavelle is the sole **black** - a relatively short descent and pales in comparison with the reds.

snowpark

A bigger snowpark than the Moonpark above Méribel it is more suited to those having a go for the first time. The flipside of this is that it is often busier. It has a better defined 4-man boardercross - complete with a starting platform - making it more of a fun-park in some ways. With 2 half-pipes and 2 quarter pipes, it has excellent terrain for getting air. One word of advice - be confident of your tricks as the park is laid out underneath the Plattières gondola so you have an airbourne audience willing you to fall.

off-piste

Mont du Vallon is home to a number of **itinerary routes** - though none are marked on the resort's official piste map. Conditions on them are generally regarded as better later on in the season - when there can be glorious spring snow. There are also plenty of off-piste shortcuts between the 2 red runs down from the peak, which make for enjoyable practise, as well as the same underneath the third stage of the Plattières gondola, the Côte Brune chairlift and the Plan des Mains chair. If you decide to venture off-piste take notice of the avalanche warnings.

eating & drinking

la sitelle (t 0479 004348) is the slope-side equivalent of a motorway service station - used mainly for pit and loo stops. On the left side of the main blue run down into Mottaret, its large terrace is too far into the shadow of the mountain to get any afternoon sun.

Both self- and table service are on offer in **le mont de la chambre** (t 0479 006768), a higgledy-piggledy place at the top of the Côte Brune chair and the junction to Val Thorens. And after a ride on the aforementioned and cruelly exposed lift you may well need to worship at the temple of the goddess of hot chocolate - available from the bar just inside the entrance. Food from both sections is consistently good value.

le roc des 3 marches (t 0479 004648) is a standard self-service at the top of the Plattières gondola. Though it has a terrace, you are unlikely to use it thanks to its exposed position.

le chalet de togniat (t 0479 004511) at the bottom of the Roc de Tougne draglift above Mottaret is a good and generally quiet restaurant with a pleasant terrace.

This area is a haven for tupperware lovers, with **picnic** spots galore - surprising given that it suffers most from bad, bad weather. There are 4 official sites to unwrap your ham butties - at the bottom of the Mont du Vallon gondola, at the top of the second stage of the Plattières gondola, at the top of the Côte Brune chairlift and at the top of the Roc de Tougne 1 & 2 button lifts. When the sun disappears behind the ridge-line in the mid-afternoon, it leaves nothing but shade and nowhere to linger.

getting home

For getting back to Méribel or Mottaret the Plan des Mains chair is the link between the Mont du Vallon peak and the pistes home - if you are too late to catch this lift the flat Ours run is a tiring alternative. From the top of the chair the home run to Mottaret is blue. Those staying in Méribel should also head to Mottaret from where you can ski down the green Truite run. If you have time you can head back up the Saulire or Tougnète side of the valley and then ski down to the village. If you plan to return by lift you can hop onto the Plattières gondola at the top of the Plan des Mains chairlift - the bottom of the gondola is in Mottaret. If you wish to continue your journey to Méribel by lift, take the Pas du Lac up and then the Burgin gondola down.

The Méribel valley is well linked to the Courchevel valley - from both La Chaudanne and Mottaret a gondola takes you to the top of the Saulire peak the highest point of the ridge between the 2 valleys. The pistes from the top run down towards the 1850 resort and towards the lift links to the skiing above 1650 (➥ 1650). The descent towards 1850 isn't for beginners as it's straight into some fairly serious skiing - a dazzling choice of reds and blacks all with a great bird's eye view of the much-used Courchevel Altiport and the whole valley below. Here too will you find the start of the infamous rock-encased Courchevel couloirs, only one of which is a piste, Le Grand Couloir. Lower down, as the mountainside falls away in a concave shape, the pistes become more forgiving, changing in grading to blue and green. With the Courchevel's perfectionism for grooming pistes, if you catch the first lift up, you can ski them at their smoothest.

access

From Méribel take the Burgin gondola. From Mottaret, take the Pas du Lac.

pistes

All of the pistes below the bottom of the Saulire cable car are **green** - pleasant, gentle slopes through the forest which all merge at the Croisette (1850's centre). Skiers who would like to try them and don't want to confront the fairly tricky red and black pistes at the top, can take the Saulire cable car down

map b

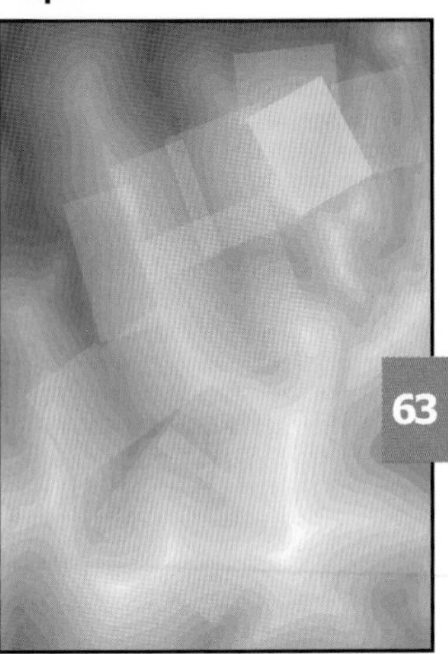

snapshot

out of interest
highest point - 2738m
aspect - n
pistes - rolling greens, connecting blues, long and lovely reds & testing blacks
off-piste - the couloirs, the creux bowl & lots of piste-side patches
restaurants - 6

highlights & hotspots
your wallet
the infamous couloirs
courchevel's snowpark
views of take-offs and landings at the altiport

to where the runs become something altogether more forgiving.

The **blues** are little to get excited about - they are blue in colour rather than spirit and could easily be classified as green. Beginners will enjoy them on the basis that they are officially harder than a green while intermediates and above will use them for little more than getting to more interesting rus.

From Saulire the runs are a mix of **reds** and blacks. The right fork at the top takes you down the long Creux and Marmottes reds which run down to the crossroads of lifts to 1850 in one direction and 1650 in the other. To the left the long Combe Saulire and Pylônes pistes under the shadow of the Saulire peak run down to the bottom of the Saulire cable car. Along the way you can watch the more advanced - or foolhardy - descending the Courchevel couloirs.

Courchevel's most infamous **black** is the Grand Couloir. Reached from the top of the Saulire cable car, the most daunting part of the experience is the approach - a traverse along a narrow ridge. Once there, the descent is similar to the nearby Suisses black run - both are covered in moguls, although the Couloir, as befits its name, is narrower, but shorter. The Suisses often offers 4 seasons in 1 dayscent - ice, moguls, powder and perfectly groomed snow.

snowpark

According to the official piste map, there are 4 in this valley. Of them, the one by the Epicéa buttonlift is the best defined, with a short boardercross course, 2 pipes (1 easy, 1 less so) and a number of jumps, tables and rails. The remaining 3 are found under the Pralong chairlift, the Biollay chairlift and the Verdons gondola and form part of the pistes - they are not sectioned off from them. They consist of little more than rolling hills (and the one under the Verdons gondola is known as the "flying carpet"), which can come as something of a surprise to beginners who think that they are a green piste.

off-piste

The obvious choices for off-piste lovers are the 2 ungroomed couloirs accessed from the top of the Saulire cable car - the one on the left as you look up to the peak is known as Télépherique while the next along is named after

Emilie Allais. The attraction of couloir skiing is the challenge of getting your turns in where needed rather than the quality of the snow - and for many its a relief to get to the bottom without getting too friendly with a rock on the way down. The forest below the bottom of the Lac Bleu draglift is one place to go when visibility is poor - but beware the tree holes and the risk of avalanche (they are often seen hurtling down the steep sides of Saulire). The bowl from the top of the Creux Noirs chairlift down towards the Creux red run is often skied, but again avalanches are a regular occurrence.

eating & drinking

In a nutshell, lunch in this area is about table-service and high prices.

Situated just above the Altiport, **cap horn** (t 0479 083310) offers sumptuous dining on the mountain. The huge terrace is warmed by gas heaters and the pleasant aspect towards the Grand Blanc peak tempts you off (the) piste. Inside the theme is nautical and cosy with a number of fireplaces, small rooms, tables at different levels and decorated throughout with a blend of wood and stone. Food ranges from the sublime to the ridiculously expensive seafood platter for 2 at €110. And should you be sadistically inclined, you can choose your preferred crustacean from the fish tank and your preferred liquid vintage from the visible and impressive wine cellar.

Those who think **le chalet de pierres** (t 0479 081861) belongs to a group of Peters will realise the real translation when they see it. Situated on the edge of the green (Verdons) piste the "chalet of stones" has a large terrace, facing the majestic Saulire peak - and for less sunny days there is a covered and heated balcony. The highlight for many is the "buffet de patisseries" which has on average 30 delicious puds to choose from each day - and as the lunch service lasts until 4pm you can take your time to enjoy it. With an average spend per head of €50, it is one of the most expensive lunch spots on the mountain. Those with smaller wallets should look underneath the main restaurant to the small **le plage** snack-stop - a stone's throw away but a world apart.

At the top of the Saulire cable car **le panoramic** (t 0479 080088) at 2723m is the valley's highest restaurant and has something to suit all tastes. There is a small kiosk selling drinks and snacks for those allergic to wasting precious skiing time. For the less impatient, there is a self-service restaurant (with indoor and outdoor seating) and a table service restaurant on the upper level for those who believe a skiing holiday is as much about it being a holiday as it is about being able to ski.

Taking its name from an aircraft popular for flying in the Alps, **le pilatus** (t 0479 082049) shares a similar aspect to the

Cap Horn, with a view over Grand Blanc - though the food and ambience in this recently renovated mountain chalet is more low-key. A deceptively large restaurant, you can choose to eat on the sunny facing terrace, or indoors in the many rooms or the ugly greenhouse room - its saving grace being the unimpeded view of the arrivals and departures at the nearby altiport.

l'arc en ciel (t 0479 083809) at the top of the Verdons gondola is a basic self-service with a hatch for take-away snacks. Opening hours can be unpredictable.

la bergerie (t 0479 082470) on the edge of the Bellecôte piste has a wonderful slope-side terrace. By day, you can enjoy the delicious food (such as grilled wild salmon) on the sun-warmed terrace and then slump on the inviting sun loungers, before ambling the short distance down the piste to the resort. Though originally used to house sheep - hence the name - you can be assured that the interior is now altogether more salubrious.

For those who want to DIY there is a **picnic** room at the bottom of the Saulire cable car. On a sunny day, there are fewer better places to sit than at the top of the Creux Noir chairlift. With a plateau at the top, it is the perfect place to enjoy the 360° view, while munching on a baguette.

getting home

Once you reach the top of the Saulire cable car (or the top of the Vizelle gondola) home on skis to Méribel is down a blue or red and to Mottaret is down a red. It's as easy to get home by lift as it is to get there. If you are as low down as the Croisette take the Verdons gondola, followed by the Saulire cable car. Then to Méribel take the Burgin gondola down and to Mottaret take the Pas du Lac gondola.

The eastern side of the Courchevel valley is home to a good selection of pistes and a less pretentious resort life. The runs above the resort are beginner friendly (a collection of greens and blues) though novices staying in Méribel will struggle to negotiate the long reds that must be skied to reach them. In comparison intermediates will find plenty to keep them entertained.

access

As for getting to the skiing above Courchevel 1850, the starting point from Méribel is the Burgin gondola to the Saulire peak - and from Mottaret it is the Pas du Lac gondola. At the top of Saulire, follow the red (Creux) run to the Chanrossa chair - which takes you to 1650's higher slopes. If you carry on down Creux to its end you can take the Roc Mugnier or Prameruel chairlifts which come out at a slightly lower point on the 1650 pistes.

pistes

The only **green** runs are immediately above the resort, useful only to get to the Ariondaz gondola and go back up again. Any beginners who've got this far in search of them needn't be looking for green.

blue runs abound in the higher environs, including the 3-line Pyramide, Mont Russe and Plan Mugnier runs, which are rolling hills, suitable for speedsters who want to get some air without too steep a landing. It's hard

map a

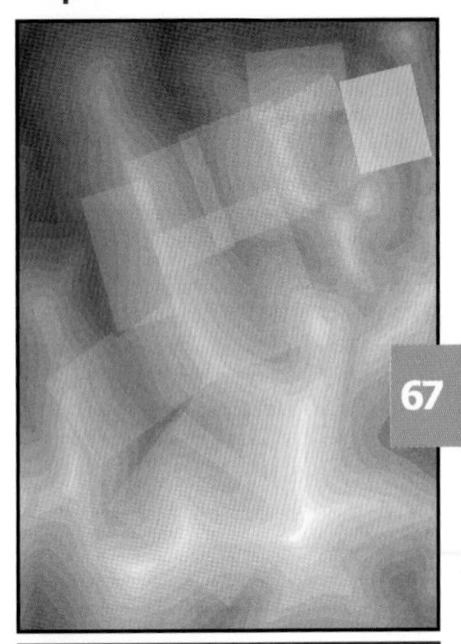

snapshot

out of interest
highest point - 2700m
aspect - e, n, w
pistes - greens lower down, speedy blues, fantastic reds & 1 black
off-piste - moguls under the chanrossa chair, les vallée des avals
restaurants - 2

highlights & hotspots
the bel air restaurant
the chapelets and rochers reds
only has chairlift access from the rest of the valley
often quiet pistes
chez le gaulois for lunch

not to add your own zoom, zoom sound effects as you cruise these motorways.

The **reds** (Chapelets, Rochers and Bel Air) at the easternmost edge of the Courchevel valley are probably the best in the valley. All are long enjoyable descents and are often over-looked and often left ungroomed after a snowfall - so those who bother can have them to themselves and may find powder. The red (Combe Roc Mugnier) on the other side of the area tends to be busier, and consequently has poorer conditions overall.

The only **black** is the Chanrossa - from the top of the chairlift of the same name. Conditions can be variable - through ice, moguls and slush.

off-piste

The area under the Chanrossa chair is popular - not least because it is easily accessed. Often mogulled, the snow conditions rarely find an equilibrium between icy and cruddy in the morning and slushy and over-skied by the afternoon - but it is an enjoyable spectacle for the audience on the Chanrossa chair. Further afield, and for the more advanced, the Vallée des Avals offers a number of descents the start of which are reached at the top of the Chanrossa chairlift - none of them should be attempted without a guide.

eating & drinking

The best place for a cheap and quick lunch is in the village itself - **chez le gaulois** serves impossibly delicious baguettes stuffed with local ham (jambon cru) and hot raclette cheese.

On the piste, **le bel air** (t 0479 080093) at the top of the Ariondaz gondola is a large, sunny chalet, which makes the most of its aspect with a 3-tiered terrace. The food is consistently good and despite the chalet's reasonable size, reservations are generally a good idea.

Offering similar fare to Le Bel Air, **la casserole** (t 0479 080635) has always lost out to its nearest rival because of its appearance. Plans are afoot to transfer the presently ugly, low-lying building into a more aesthetically pleasing wooden chalet with a terrace, to make the most of what sun gets to its position on the edge of the forest, and to tempt customers in to enjoy cuisine that is just as good.

For an indoor **picnic** head to the *salle hors sac* by the lift pass office at the bottom of the 3 Vallées chair.

getting home

As for 1850 you need to get to the top of Saulire to get home to Méribel and Mottaret - the lift to catch is the Marmottes chair from the bottom of the Chanrossa lift. From the top it is the same journey on skis or by lift.

The west flank of the Courchevel valley is often overlooked - the majority of skiers heading straight up to the Saulire peak or east to 1650. But it has plenty to offer - there are enough runs at the easy level for competent beginners and at the other end of the scale experts will delight in the Jean Blanc and Jockeys blacks. And it is an area of contrast - the view from the top of the Col de la Loze down the Méribel valley has a stunning backdrop of peaks, while lower down the tree-lined slopes are Alpine forests at their best.

access

The most direct route from Méribel as the lifts ride is up to the Col de la Loze plateau on the Loze chairlift which starts just above the Altiport. From Mottaret you can make your way to Méribel and take the same route or take the Pas du Lac gondola to the top of Saulire and make your way over using the pistes and lifts above 1850.

pistes

There is a series of **greens** from the top of the Chenus gondola - they are used for little more than getting to other steeper runs unless you are a beginner getting your money's worth out of a 3 Vallées lift pass.

The **blue** (Les Folyères) run down through the dense forest to La Tania is the kind of run that can make you feel like a champion - straight and speedy, it's a whole lot of fun. The other blue of

map c

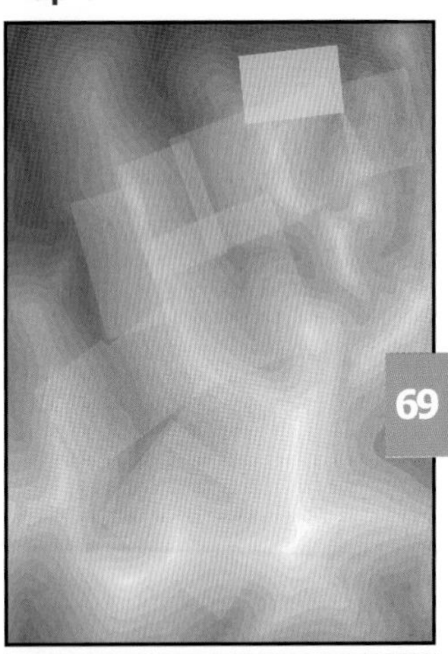

snapshot

out of interest
highest point - 2274 m
aspect - e, n, w
pistes - speedy blues, steep reds & the best blacks in the valley
off-piste - moguls under the dou des lanches chair
restaurants - 4

highlights & hotspots
the old racing runs of jockeys and jean blanc
lower slopes are often bare and unskiable
pretty tree-lined runs
steep draglifts tricky for boarders

note (Boulevard Arolles) couldn't be more different - a meandering path, it at least allows newcomers to skiing to feel like they have covered some ground. And they're unlikely to be disturbed.

The **reds** are not as plentiful as those at the top of 1850, but they are often quieter. The Dou des Lanches and Lanches runs generally have better conditions than those lower down the mountain.

The 2 **blacks** (Jockeys and Jean Blanc) are both long and testing and a lot of fun when the snow is good. Both runs finish in Le Praz. The Jockeys run joining the red (Murettes) piste to end by Le Praz's lift station. The Jean Blanc surprisingly ends in the middle of a field - you have to navigate a few back gardens to get to the village, before crossing the main road to Le Praz's lift station. For most of the season, you should expect the bottom of both to be bare in patches often with branches poking through the snow, but after a heavy snowfall experts don't need to look much further.

off-piste

In this area there is plenty of opportunity to pop off the side of the pistes and dip your booted toe into the powder. The trees in the forests between the Forêt gondola and La Tania gondola have enough space between them to execute some tidy turns -

though if there is one time you should wear a helmet it is when you are tree-skiing. For lengthier descents, there are a number of lines to the right of the Dou des Lanches chair - these are popular among the locals and seasonnaires and so get tracked out quickly.

eating & drinking

Aside from what's on the mountain, the horseshoe of La Tania offers a number of options, such as the Pub Le Ski Lodge. The choices are less obvious in Le Praz, not least because the lift station (and the end of all runs except the Jean Blanc) are some way from the eateries.

The mountain restaurants manage to be cheaper than those within closer range of 1850. **le bouc blanc** (t 0479 088026) is a traditional and homely restaurant at the top of the La Tania gondola. Open 11:30am-4pm it is best to book.

les chenus (t 0479 080684) is one of the few self-service options on this side of the Saulire ridgeline - and it manages to rise above the general expectations. At the top of the Chenus gondola (which starts from 1850's Croisette), it can also be reached by skiing along the blue from the top of the Loze chair. The food available (9am-5pm) is good regional cuisine.

Opened in 1995 **le roc tania** (t 0479 083234, i restaurants-3vallees.com), a chalet-style restaurant does a good job of looking more authentic than its young age suggests. Positioned on the flat Col de la Loze plateau between Méribel and Courchevel it has a fantastic south-west facing terrace, which gets the last rays of the day. The views are fantastic - of the mountains and the parapenters launching from up here. Open 9am-5pm, it is also a good place to stop for après to catch the last rays of the day and watch the sun sink behind the Belleville ridgeline before skiing back to resort.

la soucoupe (t 0479 082134) occupies the site of the first altitude restaurant (Relais de la Loze) in the Courchevel valley. Self-service is available - a bar and pastries for morning, and lunch from 12pm - but the restaurant on the first floor is the reason to go, and bookings are a good idea. Delightfully rustic if you opt for a steak you can watch it being grilled on the open fire and keep yourself toasty.

getting home

Home to Méribel Centre and Le Rond-Point is along a blue (Boulevard de la Loze). If you're staying near the Altiport, in Méribel Village or Morel the red (Pic Noir) comes out just above the Altiport from where you can ski home. For Mottaret or the other parts of Méribel you will have take a further lift once you are over the ridgeline. To get home by lift to either Méribel or Mottaret you need to get to the Saulire cable car (or if you're lower down the Verdons gondola from 1850's Croisette). And if you're going to do that you may as well ski home. If you are as far down as 1550, the Grangettes gondola takes you up to the Croisette.

If the 3 Vallées were the setting for a fairytale, St. Martin de Belleville would be Cinderella and Val Thorens and Les Menuires the ugly sisters. An old and charming village, and the lowest resort in the Belleville valley, there is the sense of it having been home to a community long before the hordes of winter pleasure seekers descended. From the top of the Tougnète ridge the view is of a series of gently rolling ski fields - the snow disguises what is actually grazing pasture and as you descend the mountain you pass ramshackled farmers' huts.

access

The pistes down to the village are most easily reached from La Chaudanne by the Tougnète gondola. From Mottaret the Plattières gondola takes you to the top of the Roc des 3 Marches from where you can descend towards St. Martin (or Les Menuires).

pistes

The pistes are few in number and scary is not a word that would be used to describe them - but their length make up for their scarcity and the scenery more than compensates for their moderation. **green** is not a colour that appears on the piste map, though there are enough **blues** to keep beginners or nervous intermediates happy. The long Liaison/Gros Tougne is best avoided by boarders who will become frustrated with the narrowness and level gradient of the path - even skiers may need to

map g

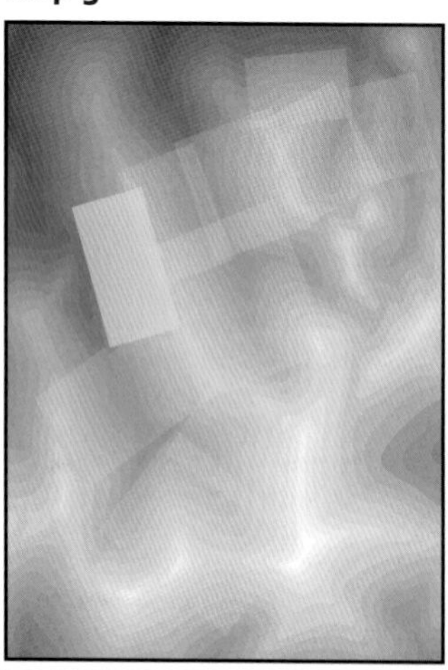

snapshot

out of interest
highest point - 2704m
aspect - w
pistes - no greens, long blues, rolling reds & no blacks
off-piste - gently sloped snowfields
restaurants - 2

highlights & hotspots
quiet pistes
the charming village of st. martin
the michelin starred la bouitte
the boring liaison and gros tongue blues
the lengthy and exciting jerusaleum red

pole in places - unless they are attempting to get to Les Menuires. All of the **reds** are found up high - the highlight is Jerusaleum, a rarely busy and always enjoyable descent that normally has good conditions.

off-piste

From the top of the Olympic chair the gentle gradient of wide open snowfields makes it ideal for leisurely off-piste skiing - though watch out for sudden drops in the terrain (cliffs!) and don't venture too far beyond the right extent of the area, or you face a long trek back to civilisation.

eating & drinking

The village of St. Martin offers some lovely spots for lunch, most noticeably **le grenier** at the hotel St. Martin - and if you have time, the charming village is worth exploring. But make sure you don't miss your lift home, as it's a costly (time and money) journey home by road. Those seeking something to remind themselves of home should try **brewski's**, known for its pies and chicken curry. For a truly gastronomic Michelin-starred lunch take the off-piste route down to the hamlet of Saint-Marcel and head for the **la bouitte** (t 0479 089677) - the restaurant will send a minibus to pick you up from the roadside at Saint-Martin if conditions are not good enough to ski to the door.

On the way down the mountain you pass **les crêtes** (➥ tougnète) while further down still, where the top of the St. Martin 1 gondola meets the bottom of the St. Martin 2 chairlift you will find **le chardon bleu** (t 0479 089536) and **le corbeleys** (t 0479 089531). Both are rustic in appearance - having had former lives as mountain huts - and serve similar ranges of Bellevilloises and Savoyarde specialities. On the last stretch of the blue run down to St. Martin you pass the large-terraced **la loë** (t 0479 089272), which serves cheap omelettes and salads.

getting home

For Méribel the St. Martin 2 chairlift takes you to the top of Tougnète from where you can get home on skis to La Chaudanne and Les Allues or by lift (the Tougnète gondola) to La Chaudanne. To get to Mottaret it's a fairly tricky ski down a red or an easy gondola (Plattières) ride from the point known as Roc des Trois Marches - you can also ski down (red or black).

A modern purpose-built resort, Les Menuires is a interesting mix of architectural designs. Following the mixed reaction to the post-modernist church the architects of the newer buildings have taken some lessons from its prettier neighbours, constructing wooden chalets instead of monolithic tower-block monstrosities - though the damage to the skyline has already been done. A favourite with families, the layout of the ski area has convenience in mind - the lifts run up the hill in a series of vertical lines and the numerous pistes run down in a similar fashion to merge in a tangled mess above the resort centre.

access

The Belleville valley runs almost parallel to the Méribel valley, but it is easier to reach Les Menuires from Mottaret, though the slopes down to the resort are red or black. From Méribel the top of the Tougnète gondola comes out at the start of the most direct route to Les Menuires - the aptly named Gros Tougne, a long and boring blue which is flat in places. From Mottaret you can reach the pistes above Les Menuires by taking the Plattières gondola to the very top or by coming off at the second station and taking the Côte Brune chairlift. Those who don't feel confident enough to ski the runs at the top can always descend towards Les Menuires in the Bruyères gondola - blue pistes are accessible from its mid-station.

map h

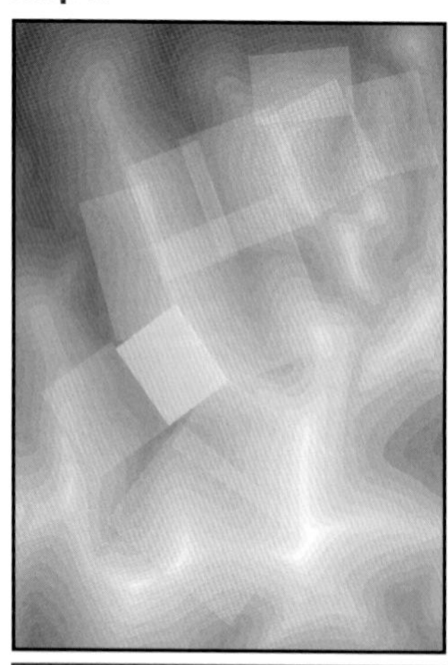

snapshot

out of interest
highest point - 2850m
aspect - w
pistes - mini greens, safe-as-houses blues, numerous and lengthy reds & surprisingly tricky blacks
off-piste - limited
restaurants - 6

highlights & hotspots
the views
the long and boring access piste from méribel
the covered mont de la chambre chair
chaotic slopes during school holidays

pistes

The few **greens** are at resort level, as are the majoirty of the **blues**. The quietest is generally the Mont de la Chambre at the far end of the area - it also generally has the best conditions, as the others closer to the resort suffer from over-use. The blues below the resort are worth disregarding altogether as they are little more than access pistes to the skiing on La Masse (the ski slopes on the opposite side of the valley from Les Menuires) or the small areas of acommodation below the main resort.

Of the **reds** Les 4 Vents can live up to its name, while the rest are simliar in nature - long and generally enjoyable descents that are on the top edge of the red bracket.

The **blacks** too are surprisingly tricky given the family-tastic nature of the resort. All can be icy but they are seldom busy.

off-piste

As so much of this area is groomed even the piste-side off-piste is limited. If that is what you are looking for you should head down the valley to St. Martin or back over the ridge to Méribel.

eating & drinking

There are plenty of pit-stops in the resort itself, most of which are ideally placed on the side of the piste, so you don't have to venture too far from the snow. One of them is the English-run **sphère** bar and restaurant, which serves food 12pm-3:30pm - you can also check your emails at their internet station if you don't like being out of touch for too long.

les quatre vents (t 0479 006444) on the hill is decorated throughout with stuffed animals eerily preserved as if mid-movement - which can be a little disconcerting as you tuck into your frites - though the the advert outside suggests this menagerie is something the restaurant is proud of. Once you get accustomed to their glassy stares the reasonably good self-service food (and good made-to-order omelettes) is reasonably priced and the staff are friendly.

The **chalet du capricorne** (t 0479 006510) just below Les Menuires provides architectural relief from the rest of the resort - a small slope-side cabin on the blue piste down towards La Masse/Le Bettex - the menu is similar to what you find elsewhere.

getting home

As for 'access' it is easier to get home through Mottaret. The Mont de la Chambre chair and the Bruyères gondola both end at the top of Mont de la Chambre and the top of the main descent to Mottaret. Returning home by lift is not an option from here. To do that you need to pass over the ridge at the Roc des 3 Marches.

La Masse is opposite Les Menuires and is the chalk to its cheese. The masses generally don't bother so there are no family-littered pistes here, just a handful of reds and blacks that are generally quiet and in generally excellent condition. One of the best destinations for intermediate and expert skiers, La Masse, being east facing, is best for morning skiing as it falls into shadow by the afternoon - though as it is some distance from Méribel you will be lucky to get there before mid morning. There are many short stretches of off-piste in between the slopes for those looking for powder. The view from the top of the highest peak is also one of the best - an expanse of further peaks and snow fields and the beginning of some of the area's most enjoyable itinerary routes. Even if you don't fancy skiing the steepish reds and blacks from the top it is worth going up for the view.

access

As La Masse lies on the far side of the Belleville valley, you first pass through Les Menuires. Look for a gap in the semi-circle of commerce at the bottom of the pistes - the piste through this gap leads down to the lift links to La Masse.

pistes

That there are no **green** pistes sums up the spirit of La Masse. The only **blue** of significance is the Vallons run from the top of the Rocher Noir chairlift - and it is generally the busiest piste in the area.

map i

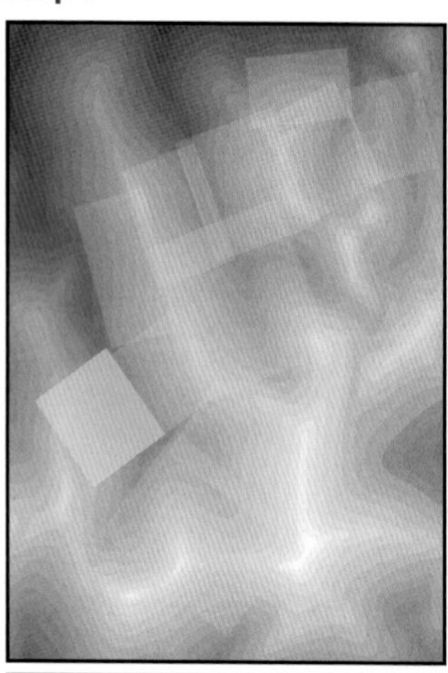

snapshot

out of interest
highest point - 2804m
aspect - e
pistes - a few blues, long and fast reds & testing blacks
off-piste - extensive itineraries & numerous powder bowls
restaurants - 3

highlights & hotspots
access to some of the area's best off-piste
consistently good snow conditions
quiet pistes
quite a trek from méribel

For **reds** you are spoilt for choice and can descend from top to bottom by red alone - up high the Fred Covill run from the top of the Masse 2 gondola, and then Les Enverses to the bottom of the Rocher Noir chair.

Of the 2 **blacks** found here the Dame Blanche has the most to offer - a steepish descent on the far right side of the area it is accessed on the Masse draglift, which is not always open. The Lac Noir from the top of the chair of the same name is probably only graded black because it is narrow.

off-piste

The off-piste accessible from the top of La Masse has the reputation of being some of the best in the area. The choice of routes is varied so you can make it as hard as you want it to be, and it is one way to get away from the manufactured feel of Les Menuires. A number of routes pass through the Vallée of Entremont which is still home to farming communities and herds of cattle - and which you may ski past (or through) during the spring months. Also from the back of La Pointe de la Masse (the area's highest point) you can reach St. Martin de Belleville by heading down the Col de Fenêtre.

eating & drinking

There are 3 options for food and drink - **le panoramic** (t 0479 228060) at the very top, **les roches blanches** (t 0479 006022) mid-way down and **les 3V** (t 0479 007404) towards the bottom. Le Panoramic is a cosy little place where you are likely to come across groups of ski adventurers about to descend into the endless off-piste down the backside of the peak. Les Roches Blanches is more of a haunt for intermediate skiers. A pleasant self-service, it has a large terrace outside from where you can admire what you have just come down. Inside there is a sweet mezzanine level where you can warm up with a plate of frites and a coke. Les 3V is also self-service, and one which upsets the stereotype. The food served is excellent - a range of hearty soups, decent slabs of French cheese and home-made puddings, all of which can be eaten on the lovely terrace on the edge of the piste.

getting home

As for Les Menuires the easiest way home is through Mottaret. At the bottom of La Masse take the Doron chair or the Croisette gondola to get back to the lifts from Les Menuires that will take you home. You can't get from the very top of La Masse to the bottom by lift - unless you fancy walking from the bottom of La Masse 2 gondola to the top of La Masse 1 gondola.

The highest resort in not only the 3 Vallées but also the European Alps, and (logically) the highest skiing in the 3 Vallées - 3200m at the top of the Cime de Caron. It is the only valley in which the pistes are on a glacier. Situated at the top end of the Belleville valley, and surrounded by a half-moon crescent of mountains, the skiing is wide and open. Its altitude makes it susceptible to changeable weather - it is not unusual to bask in sunshine in Méribel and find Val Thorens shrouded in cloud - so dress warm. The link between the valleys closes at the first puff of a breeze. Val Thorens is not for the aesthete: the area is desolate without a tree in sight - and compared to the picture postcard charm of Méribel the resort is something of a monstrosity.

In recent years the valley over the ridge from Cime de Caron has been tamed. A great destination for those suffering from cabin fever, claustrophobia or just looking to escape from the masses - it is the only valley where you can enjoy the feeling of quiet isolation without the extra challenge of being off-piste. On a clear day the views are stunning with very little urbanisation in sight. During a good season, you can ski down to the small village of Orelle.

access

The skiing above Val Thorens is the least easy to reach. The resorts of Courchevel and Méribel lie vaguely parallel to each other within their valley

map j & k

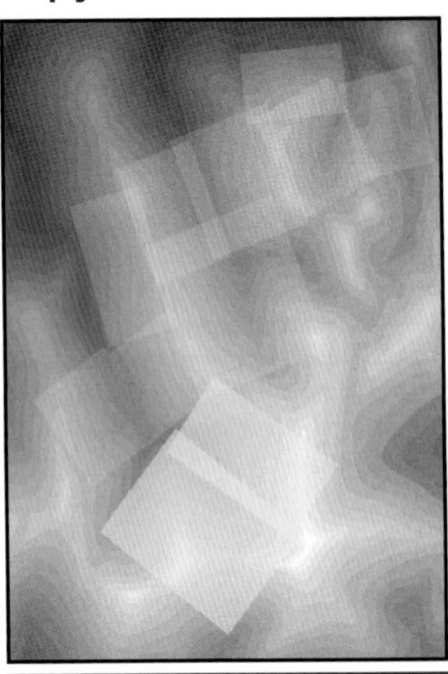

snapshot

out of interest
highest point - 3230m
aspect - all
pistes - resort-level greens, long blues, longer reds & steep or bumpy blacks
off-piste - extensive: couloirs, glaciers & bowls
restaurants - 12

highlights & hotspots
the cime de caron black
the 4th valley
susceptible to windy conditions
consequently often closed

so linkage between them is easy. Val Thorens by contrast is actually some way further away. The most direct route starts in Mottaret passing through the Mont du Vallon area. Take the Plattières gondola to its second stage, ski down the Bouvreuil run (blue or red depending upon your ability) to the bottom of the Côte Brune chairlift. This brings you out at the top of Mont de la Chambre, and the crossroads of runs back down to Mottaret and to Val Thorens. Boarders will need to get up some speed on the flat approach run from the top towards Val Thorens.

To reach Maurienne, ski through the Val Thorens resort and take the Moutière chair and then the Funitel Grand Fond - the entrance to the 4th valley is through a stone-blasted opening in the rock, which may well remind you of Harry Potter. Alternatively you can take the Caron gondola followed by the Cime de Caron cable car, though this way you are committed to skiing a black run.

pistes

The pistes immediately around Val Thorens are all **green**, which makes reaching the rest of the area child's play.

The approach runs from the Méribel valley are mainly **blue** - and all are long and fun. Those around the resort are similar, though some are flat enough to justify a green grade. The 2 blues in the 4th valley are generally enjoyable too - though the Gentianes down into the valley is track-like in places.

The valley is home to oodles of **reds**. Those on the Pèclet glacier are very popular - generally have the best conditions and such even terrain that you can reach some fairly high speeds. The reds from the Breche de Rosaël are ideal for carving practise as are those from the Boismint and Plan de l'Eau chairs, which are generally the quietest in the area.

Val Thorens is home to probably the best **black** in the 3 Vallées ski area, the long and speedy Cime de Caron. Starting at 3200m, this sweeps down under the shadow of the peak of the same name. Being reasonably sheltered and north-facing, the conditions are generally good, though susceptible to some icy patches. Over in the 4th valley the only black (Combe Rosaël) runs from the top of the Cime de Caron and had a previous existence as an itinerary route.

snowpark

The Val Thorens snowpark is small compared to those in the Méribel valley - and it is not steep enough to get any serious air. The boardercross in the 4th valley is not obviously marked nor always open, but finding your own line down it can be fun.

summer skiing

Val Thorens is one of the few resorts in

European that is open during the summer for skiing. The Pèclet glacier sees some snow 365 days a year and though the skiing is limited a summer holiday in Val Thorens is certainly different from the usual trip to the beach.

off-piste

The Val Thorens has plenty of piste-side powder - particularly around the boardercross course in the 4th valley - and it provides the start to a number of excellent off-piste **itinerary routes** and glacier skiing. At the bottom end of the valley is the Lac du Lou - the area between Val Thorens and La Masse. If you start at the top of the Cime de Caron the vertical descent is over 1000m - though pick your route at the bottom carefully and you may end up in somewhere very icy and cold. The 4th valley has enough off-piste to keep you going for the whole of your stay - to make sure you see the best of it take a guide.

eating & drinking

le chalet du thorens (t 0479 000280) is a big venture with a mass market feel. Maze-like in layout, there are enough choices to confuse even the least weather-beaten skier. Options include table-service Savoie specialities, self-services standards and take-away paninis from the stall outside.

le galoubet (t 0479 000048), in the heart of the resort, is easy to spot - its huge outdoor terrace is festooned with green umbrellas. Located on the right hand side of the resort as you ski through it you can grab a take-away sandwich on your way.

le chalet de caron (t 0479 000171) is one of the better self-service restaurants in the 3 Vallées. The choice of food is wide and reasonably priced with a good salad buffet and the usual *saucisson et frites*. There is a huge terrace outside for sunny days and an equally large seating area inside.

l'oxalys (t 0479 001200) next to Club Med's Val operation, on the side of the Cairn piste, has a south-facing terrace and a good reputation. As the chef is something of an experimenter (making interesting use of ingredients) this is not your usual slope-side eating experience - it is not unusual to find liquorice in the same dish as potatoes. And, in an otherwise cheap Val Thorens, the bill reflects the care and attention given.

la moutière (t 0479 000267) is a lovely piste-side cabin at the top of the lift of the same name. Dog lovers will delight in the very friendly resident hound.

On the Cascade piste **le bar de la marine** (t 0479 000312) is a good service restaurant with a nautical theme and an owner with a very well-tended moustache.

If you are skiing at the lower end of the valley **le chalet des 2 ours** (t 0479 011409) on the Boismint piste is more than adequate for a quick lunch. At the other extreme of the area **l'altiself 3000** (t 0479 000376) is one of the 2 places in the valley where you can have lunch on a glacier. **l'étape 3200** (t 0607 310414) is the other and takes the accolade of being the highest mountain restaurant in the whole of the 3 Vallées.

Just off the run of the same name **le chalet de genépi** (t 0479 000328) below the Moraine chair-lift has an open fire inside and good views from its sunny terrace.

Over in the 4th valley, the **plan bouchet refuge** (t 0479 568808) is the only lunch-stop and is proof that although the lifts are here the spirit of the rest of the 3 Vallées has yet to follow. A very basic self-service restaurant, it is likely to be filled with gnarly mountain men, rather than fur-clad Parisiennes. That said, the food fills a hole. And there is a microwave, should you have remembered to throw a ready meal into your backpack at the start of the day. It is also possible to stay the night here (and make the most of having made the lengthy trip from Méribel) if you remembered to throw in a sleeping bag as well.

As you need to make a couple of lifts to get back to Méribel après around Val Thorens is not advised. And if you're in the 4th valley for après, you're in trouble on 2 counts - the venues are non-existent and you've got a long and expensive journey home. Never has "one for the road" been so literal.

getting home

There are a variety of routes home. You can go through Les Menuires - ski down the Boulevard Cumin, which links the 2 resorts. The more direct way is over the Col de la Chambre - take the Bouquetin lift to the top. Save some energy for the journey home as there is a long ski down the Lac de la Chambre red until you reach you next lift link - the Plan des Main chair. If by then your legs have given out you can catch the Plattières gondola from its second stage back down to Mottaret.

Though you can get into the 4th valley from the top of the Cime de Caron cable car, you can only return by the Rosaël peak - there is no lift link back up to the Cime de Caron. Boarders should expect a bit of a walk from the top of the Rosaël chairlift.

And finally. If you miss the last lift take your wallet - a taxi from Val Thorens to Méribel costs a purse-shattering €140. The alternative is a slow bus journey with a change in Moûtiers.

So many pistes, so little time. Often it's difficult to know where to start, where to find the longest runs, or where to go when there's not much snow or the weather is bad. Here are a few suggestions.

the first morning

The pistes above the Altiport are a good place to stir the slumbering skiing muscles - as all are easy greens or blues. When your knees have remembered how to bend, a short trip further up the mountain takes you to the top of some slightly longer but nonetheless unthreatening blues and reds.

all-day sunshine

If it's time to tan, you can track the sun (the weather obliging) from first light to last, both on lift and on piste. Start the day on the Tougnète side, taking the Plan de l'Homme chairlift from La Chaudanne. Keeping one (sunglassed) eye on the sun, ski whichever pistes you like, using whichever lifts you like, but moving gradually towards Mont du Vallon. For lunch you can do little better than Mottaret - on sunny days the Front de Neige takes on pool-side proportions with the quantity of sun-worshippers that gather there. By the afternoon the sun will be smiling on the Saulire side of the valley, where again the pistes and lifts are yours to choose. Only one note of caution - in the sage words of Baz Luhrmann, always wear sunscreen.

a bumpy ride

If moguls are your thing, the black pistes (the Face and Les Bosses) on the Tougnète side of Méribel are both home to some fine stretches of bumps. Over in Courchevel there's nothing neutral about the pockmarks on Les Suisses.

do a figure of 8

This one takes a bit of planning and requires co-operation from the weather - then top of the list is an early start and throughout the day you should pay attention to the time of the last lift home. As the sun is only in the Courchevel valley in the morning, head there first - passing into it over the Col de La Loze plateau and returning via the Saulire peak. Put in a brief stop at Mottaret - where you can grab a take-away lunch and then head up the Plattières gondola to the Belleville valley. Once there take your pick of the pistes above St. Martin, Les Menuires or Val Thorens. Wherever you decide to descend, remember to give yourself enough time to get home - the only thing that will spoil a day exploring the full extent of the area is getting stuck in the wrong valley.

brave a cold snap

Should temperatures be close to unbearable, make full use of the valley's gondolas to get to the top of the pistes. And if you've changed your mind by the time you got to the top, you can always stay in the warmth of the fibreglass cabin and head back down for a day in bed instead.

stay out all night

Ever fancied a night on the hill? The Refuge de la Traye (t 0479 005726) at 1700m on the Tougnète side of the valley makes it possible. Only reachable by skiing off-piste (or using snowshoes) along the itinerary route down towards Les Allues, there is (cosy) bed and board for 7 people.

get an award

The resorts and the ESF have designated certain points in the 3 valleys as "must-sees" - 16 in total, listed on a "discovery card" which is available from any office of the ESF. Once your card has 16 ticks - your visits being certified by your (ESF) instructor at the end of each day - you get your very own shiny 3 Vallées medal. And though to some this may seem like a cynical ploy to get you to book lessons at least you'll have made the most of your 3 Vallées lift pass - and seen some of the most beautiful parts of the area.

bad weather

As so many of Méribel's lifts are gondolas, bad weather can halt all chances of getting up the mountain. The second stage of the Burgin lift on the Saulire side closes in high winds and the same is true for the upper part of the Tougnète gondola and the gondola lifts from Mottaret. The Loze chair may open, and the lower part of the Pic Noir run is through the trees, which at least offer some point of reference for the eyes. Otherwise the choice is limited. The area around the Altiport is reasonably wooded and offers some protected but limited skiing, which is fine for beginners and practising intermediates, but expert skiers would have to be desparate to bother. A better bet on a bad weather day is the resort's cinema or the leisure facilities and bars.

off-piste

Despite its fame as a skier's paradise the 3 Vallées is not the first place you'd think of for gnarly off-piste. As so much of the area is groomed there is not a huge amount of lift-accessed off-piste - you have to work a bit harder to reach the holy grail, though often a short trek is all it takes. Piste-side powder-poachers can take their pick - many runs have open space off to the side. Hikers will not find marked itineraries as in Verbier or Zermatt, but hiring a guide will reveal a world of powder trails both well known and not - and as the terrain hides a variety of cliffs, chutes and tree-holes it is by far the safest way to explore.

The best - and most easily accessed - off-piste in the Méribel valley can be found on Mont du Vallon. There are a number of itinerary routes here (not marked on the official piste map), which lead to some accessible off-piste - the most obvious is a left turning 20m from the top of the Mont du Vallon gondola. Route-finding is relatively easy and the skiing is more wide bowls than narrow couloirs. For adrenaline junkies (with ability) the couloir visible to the left of the Saulire peak as you ascend in the Burgin gondola, known as the Elevator Shaft, will get the pulse racing. Reached under the Saulire building walk along the ridge until you see a metal ladder. As the couloir is south-facing and narrow, it is best avoided after a prolonged sunny stretch and particularly heavy snow. Off-piste skiing from the Tougnète ridge is altogether more gentle in nature - head to the top of the Olympic chair for the start of a number of descents which lower down pass through the scenic forests and past seemingly forgotten mountain huts. On the other side of the Saulire ridgeline, the obvious choices for lift-accessed off-piste are the Emilie Allais and Télépherique couloirs - warm up first on the pisted and somewhat wider Grand Couloir. Further along the ridge are the even steeper Curé couloir and the even less accessible Verdons Cross couloir. As with any off-piste skiing, the usual precautions should be taken. It's all very well having a brand spanking new Dakine backpack if you don't know how to use the contents (transceiver, shovel and probe). For fuller descriptions of these routes see the book 'Les 3 Vallées Hors pistes - Off piste' by Philippe Baud and Benoit Loucel.

ski touring

Ever wondered about the seemingly mad bunch of skiers who walk up pistes as well as down? To the uninitiated it can seem a desparate bid to save on the lift pass, or complete disregard for a perfectly good lift system. This 'sport' is known as ski touring or ski mountaineering - on a 'tour' you travel from 'a' to 'b' in the same way as hiking up mountains in summer. Ski touring means you can get to places not accessed by lift and into off-piste territory otherwise hidden from view. And believe it or not there is immense satisfaction after a physically demanding ascent or descent as well as the enjoyment of being amidst the alpine scenery, away from the mêlée of the pistes. Obviously, different equipment is necessary. To climb up slopes you need skis with touring bindings, which unlock to allow the heel to come away from the ski as you step upwards. You also carry 'skins' - now artificial but so called because they were originally seal skins - to attach to the base of the skis during a climb to prevent them from slipping down. The same precautions that apply to off-piste skiing apply equally to touring. Though ski tourers are not as common a sight in Méribel as in resorts such as Chamonix, there is plenty to be done. For keen tourers a particularly excellent adventure is a trip to Le Refuge du Roc de la Pêche (t 0479 087975, i rocdelapeche.com). More of a retreat than a refuge (relative to the usual dormitory accommodation and cold showers) it has facilities that many resort-based hotels would envy. At 2000m close to the small resort of Pralognan and on the edge of the beautiful Vanoise National Park, there is a bar, restaurant, sauna, hammam, jacuzzi - all designed to make your stay as pleasant as possible. During the winter the refuge is accessible through La Vallée de Chavière - reached most easily from Val Thorens. The journey starts at the top of the Col chairlift above Val Thorens and a 2-hour skin climb to the Col de Gebrolaz (3434m) to ski on the Glacier de Gebroulaz. Because you're on a glacier, a guide is essential to avoid the numerous crevasses. The glacier faces mainly north so the snow is more often than not powdery and light. Some previous off-piste and touring experience is advised. And be sure to arrive before 7pm if you intend to stay the night.

events

The Méribel valley is no Verbier when it comes to winter events - though you won't find too many sponsored pro-riders or any world championship fixtures, you may get the chance to see skiers hurtle down a near-vertical ski jump or packs of dogs hurtling through the forest.

One of the most spectacular events is held over the ridge in Courchevel. The **courchevel freeride championship** is when top-class skiers descend the Rocher de la Loze (the peak above the Col de la Loze plateau). Best enjoyed with a picnic and a camera.

If the timing of your trip coincides with a **ski jump** competition, it is worth making the visit to Le Praz in Courchevel. The impressive jump there was built for the 1992 winter Olympics in Albertville and watching skiers whizzing down it will make you realise Eddie 'the Eagle' Edwards wasn't that bad after all. The question most ask, is how do you know you can do it?

The **3 vallées rally** at the end of the season is a team event for pros, amateurs and children. A series of races (derbies, skiercross, free-ride) is held throughout the area - contact the tourist office for more details.

One of the most popular events is the "Savoy Tropy", an international **dogsled race**. A 4-stage event (the other 3 stages are held elsewhere) over 50 teams of beautiful blue-eyed dogs and not-so-beautiful men compete on the tree-lined trails around the Altiport.

The **natives workers challenge** (natives.co.uk/race) is a fun event that runs in 4 resorts across the Alps and is geared towards seasonnaires. The Méribel leg is the giant slalom. Though some participants take it seriously, most take it socially. One-weekers may as well join in the social side of the fun - and watch the skiing, if only to feel jealous.

The ice rink in the Parc Olympique often plays host to regional - and even international - **ice-hockey** matches. On a more local basis the ESF run weekly **chamois** and **flèche** tests for young and old.

activities

A holiday in the snow need not only be about down, down, down - here are a few other ideas. And to take the hassle out of it the British-run Whitetr@ks (t 0686 123417, i whitetracks.co.uk) can organise most snow-based fun for you.

The 3 Vallées has over 100kms of **cross-country** tracks, 33kms of which are in the Méribel valley, so you can cover quite a lot of ground. The tourist office publish a leaflet ("du Fond du Coeur") that describes the routes and some of the flora and fauna you may see along the way. One of the prettiest (and flattest) routes is the Bouc Blanc track running through the forest between the Plantrey chairlift just below Courchevel 1850 passing above La Tania to the altiport in Méribel. The ESF run a programme of cross-country ski days - and lessons for those who are unsure of their technique. **snowshoeing** is an alternative way to discover the area - and one of the only ways that you can visit the stunning Rueda nature reserve at the foot of Mont du Vallon. The ESF or Raquette Evasion (t 0479 241040, i raquettevasion.com) run organised and themed tours. Raquette Evasion will also arrange torchlit tramps or overnight excursions. If you want to strike out on your own you can pick up a trail map from the tourist office and hire a pair of shoes from the bigger sports shops.

If you feel enthused after watching the "Savoy Trophy" you can try **dog-sledding** yourself, for 2 hours, a half day or a nightime jaunt. The dogs (and their owners) are based in Méribel Village - book through Traîneau Evasion (t 0479 088155/0680 631572).

As **heliskiing** is forbidden by law in France, you are better saving your cash until you find yourself in a resort such as Verbier or Zermatt or better still North America. If you are determined to fly-ski you can organise a trip through the Bureau des Guides.

After the lifts close in Mottaret you can take to the slopes by **ski doo** - book through Snow-biker (t 0479 003112, i snow-biker.com). **torchlit descents** are also held on the slopes above Mottaret - starting at 5:30pm every Wednesday, book through the Mottaret tourist office.

the resorts

When you're not on the slopes, how hectic your holiday is depends very much on which resort you are staying in. Though most of the **restaurants** are French owned a lot of the food is Italian themed - it's easy to come by big plates of carbohydrate with which to replace calories lost on the slopes. It's a blessing the Italians came up with the idea of tomatoes and cheese on a doughy base or there would be slim pickings for dinner. Savoyarde food (fondue, tartiflette, braserade, pierre chaude and raclette) is also fairly inescapable. If you are keen to try one of the Savoie recipes make sure you take a friend, as without exception they can only be ordered for a minimum of 2 people. Unlike over the valley in Courchevel the altitude of your fondue has little effect on the price. The only non-French or non-pizza alternative is Tex-Mex at the aptly named Cactus Café. As most visitors stay in chalets, they only have 1 evening meal to think about and shouldn't feel too constrained by the choice. Bookings are only essential mid-week when the chalet girls and boys have their night off. If you're feeling peckish long before supper time, it's not hard to get your hands in a decent piece of cake (it being France) - the difficult bit is choosing which 1 (or 3) to eat. As the Méribel valley is fairly narrow and lies between 2 ridges, you will find most of the restaurants in Centre aren't much of a sun-trap. So lunching *al fresco* is best done up the mountain.

In the following reviews the restaurants have a price rating, based on the average price of a main course per head excluding drinks.
£ - under €9
££ - €9-13
£££ - €13-17
££££ - €18-21
£££££ - over €21

Méribel's **après** and **nightlife** does not show much of a pattern - though it is a good example of how ski resorts are now about business, and less about a local family running a local bar for local people. Dick's Tea-Bar, La Taverne, Pizza Express, Le Pub and Le Rond-Point are all owned by the same (English) company, while a English duo own and run the triumverate of Barometre, Fix and Jack's. In most places you can get the 7% proof Mutzig beer - the stuff of a real alpine hangover - and cocktails are also becoming a regular fixture on the menu. On the mountain Méribel has more of a après scene than Courchevel, though this is concentrated in 1 or 2 well-visited places. Back down in the village most of the bars are closed by 1:30am, when you have the choice of 2 nightclubs.

snapshot

the best

The ingredients of most people's ideal ski holiday are pretty easy to pin down. You need mountains, and snow, good company, friendly locals, hearty après, stodgy food, some late night revelry and an early morning headache. Accordingly, along with being in the right location, ski resorts tend to provide liberal doses of fondue and beer and let your holiday spirit organise the rest. If you like to go home in the knowledge you've been to the best the area has to offer read on...

The choice for breakfast is surprisingly wide - hot and tasty baguettes from **la taverne**, classic French croissants and pastries from **boulangerie les glaciers**. The best restaurants for traditional French food are found along the winding road up through the suburbs. **chez kiki's** menu oozes true blue steaks while at **les enfants terribles**, slightly further up the road, you can gorge on *escargots* and *foie gras*. For back-to-basics eating and surrounds, **le plantin** (just past Méribel Village on the road to La Tania) is a fun experience - though be careful not to annoy the fiesty hostess. For more serene Savoyarde dining **chez from'ton** in the Centre never fails to deliver a perfect fondue - and in Mottaret **la brizolée** oozes rustic charm as well as cheese. For something to fill the gap between lunch and dinner, **bibi phoque crêperie** near La Chaudanne offers an extensive range of galettes and crêpes or it's back to the **boulangerie** for beyond tasty coffee cream eclairs or any number of delicious pastries. In Mottaret the under-recommended **la vieille crêperie** has a similar pancake based menu plus more ice-cream than a Ben & Jerry's outlet.

If you're more concerned with drinking, English-dominated après is easy to come by. **le rond-point** is the place to go for live music with your first drink, while **le pub** takes over the baton later on the evening. Best chance of a seat is at **barometre** and best chance of a hangover is among **le pub's** extensive range of flavoued vodkas, closely followed by **jack's** and **la taverne**. The tiny **le saint amour** has the widest range of grape-based offerings - and the most French welcome and feel - while **le poste de secours** is the leader of the pack for cocktails (and high prices). The late night choice is restricted to 2 options in Méribel - **dick's** for seasonnaires and school-girl silliness and **le loft** for leopard print and lotharios - and the underground **privilège** in Mottaret.

The heart of the heart and where you will find the bulk of everything but accommodation. While most people stay in the suburbs or in the small satellite villages scattered through the valley, most of them shop, eat and play in Centre. At the bottom is La Chaudanne: home to the lift pass office, a large covered car park and the Parc Olympique - the enduring and not-so-pretty remains of the 1992 Winter Olympics. Moving up the hill takes you past the Tremplin complex - the first clump of pubs, shops and restaurants. A little further up is the main square, home to the tourist office, the ESF office and the post office, and the point for New Year and other celebrations. The upper road above the square is lined with a 2-tiered walkway (Galerie des Gentianes and Galerie des Cimes) of more shops and restaurants, including a supermarket. All aspects considered Centre is actually quite small - the distance between La Chaudanne and the main square is little more than a 10 minute walk at a leisurely pace. Mussillon, the name given to the small road-side hamlet just below Centre, is even smaller. Little more than a cheaper option for the UK tour operators who run chalets in Méribel, it is a curious mix of old French and new British. French and old are the ramshackle collection of stone buildings and the cute and colourful chapel, while British and new are the branch of Pizza Express, the logoed 4WDs and the reliably English Dick's Tea-Bar.

<< eating out >>

For cheese lovers, no visit to the Savoie region would be complete without a fondue - and Chez From'ton serves the best. Beneath La Fromagerie shop you are assured of an excellent meal of delicious cheese served in suitably local surroundings - the heady aroma that greets you as you enter the shop whets the appetite for what the kitchen below can produce. Those who like a bit of mystery should try the namesake fondue - not even bribery will tempt the maître d' to reveal the secret ingredient. Despite being underground the room is surprisingly ambient and airy enough to prevent that lovely aroma from lingering.

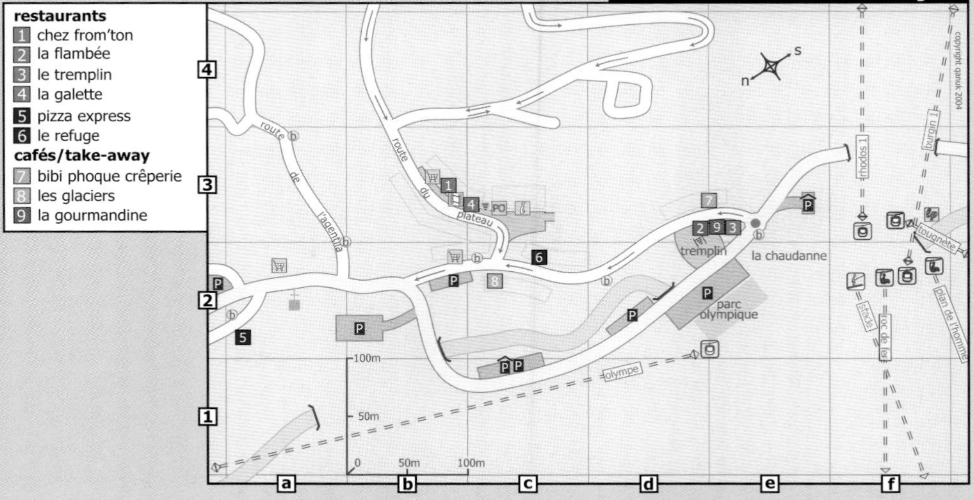

méribel centre & mussillon eating out

restaurants

1 chez from'ton
2 la flambée
3 le tremplin
4 la galette
5 pizza express
6 le refuge

cafés/take-away

7 bibi phoque crêperie
8 les glaciers
9 la gourmandine

copyright qanuk 2004

route de l'agentria
route du plateau
tremplin
la chaudanne
parc olympique
olympe
rhodos 1
burgin 1
tougnète
plan de l'homme
roc de fer
stade
0 50m 100m

Not a canny Frenchman passing off the well-known English chain, but an actual branch. The gastronmically weary or the home-sick will be relieved that the menu is exactly the same, so you can tuck into your favourite fiorentina. Otherwise there may be some differences to your local Express back home - such as regular live music, from Beatles tribute bands to jazz pianists that get the crowd dancing on the tables as the evening and the flow of wine progresses. Also if you eat here you get free entry to Dick's Tea-Bar next door (➥ après-ski & nightlife).

Tucked away at the upper end of the Centre, a number of factors might tempt you in. The first is the good food - well-stuffed galettes and crêpes and extremely filling pizzas overloaded with interesting toppings - try the cream, bacon, potatoes, onions and reblochon cheese topped 'Méribeloise'. Another is the ambience - relaxed enough for a casual lunch during the day and formal enough to feel special at night and French enough to make you forget that there is a White Stuff shop a couple of doors down. Staff are friendly, though they sometimes take their socialising too far and often give chatting to friends priority over dealing with diners - but with everything else going for this cosy little eaterie, that is a minor quibble.

Occupying a long stretch of the walkway just below Centre's main square, this family run place has 2 levels and 2 faces. The ground floor restaurant serves pizzas and crêpes from 3:30pm (which you can also take away). Upstairs is higher in venue and prices, more formal in style and more gourmet in menu - those looking for something other than pizza will enjoy the generally well-cooked fish and meat dishes. It is closed Sundays.

Another restaurant that wears 2 hats, taking tips for its food from both France and Italy. Though Savoyarde dishes are available it is not a pure local place and the pizzas are some of the best dishes (which you can also take away). If you can't decide between the two you can always have the best of both worlds with a pizza Savoyarde.

The Gallic equivalent of an English greasy spoon, this steamy little caff is the perfect place to ease your hangover or to hide from a blizzard. Serving crêpes and galettes - presumably the French answer to a fry-up - the service is charming and friendly. And in a welcome change from most eateries in Méribel, it is as likely to be frequented by Gauloise toting locals as hungry skiers.

Centre's only proper tea-room, Les Glaciers doesn't only deal in cake. If you are fending for yourself in an apartment you will be pleased to know it does a breakfast menu, and for lunch you can have delicious salads and sandwiches. As you have to pass through the boulangerie downstairs to get to the tea-room you'll have probably chosen your dessert before you see the menu. The tea-room is a bit lacking in character and is slightly sterile, but it is rarely over-busy. And surroundings aren't generally a concern when you trying to replace those calories burnt up on the mountain - and more.

Takng the best all-round eaterie prize, not only is Le Tremplin open for breakfast, lunch and dinner, but it is also one of the best places to take the kids - the waiters won't blink if you just order an ice-cream at midday. And as one of the closest restaurants to La Chaudanne it won't be too much of an ordeal to get them there.

and the rest

An alternative option for a crêpe is the **grand marnier crêperie** outlet, just a short walk from La Chaudanne - just don't expect to get one without the name-sake liqueur. For a take-away breakfast **la taverne** (➥ après-ski & nightlife) sells tasty, hot rolls, while for lunch the **bakery** below Les Glaciers has sandwiches in addition to a mouth-watering range of cakes. For something hot and moveable **la gourmandine** in the Tremplin complex sells tasty and well-filled paninis. For late-night snacks make sure you stock up before the supermarket closes - there is nowhere open past the witching hour.

<< après-ski & nightlife >>

le saint amour

p97 b3

0479 003527

4pm-1:30am

This tiny wine bar is refreshingly individual compared to the more formulaic atmosphere in some of Méribel's other watering holes. Choose from a huge selection of French white and red wines which the delightful and knowledgeable hostess spends her summers sourcing and is more than happy to chat about at length. Though the high wooden stools perched around the counter look less than comfy, the hours will pass by without notice in an increasingly bacchanalian haze.

fix

The newest of the English-run trio and the up-market end of the triangle - a chilled out venue of leather sofas, opulent dark red walls and a long and lovely cocktail list. Though there are few seats there's plenty of leaning room at the bar - and it's rarely as busy as Jack's next door. Fix serves as well as somewhere for an afternoon coffee as it does for an evening drink (with a cleverly timetabled happy hour 10:30pm-11:30pm) and opens at at 12pm on bad weather days.

jack's

While Fix aims for quiet sophistication Jack's plumps for liveliness and fun - perhaps helped by the 7% Mutzig on tap and a not-so-secret secret ingredient (grand marnier) in the vin chaud. A well established favourite with the party crowd, the critical eye may think it needs a face-lift, but the clientele don't seem to object and with the same late happy hour as Fix (10:30pm-11:30pm) you may not feel the need to move on.

barometre

The third and most central of the trio, and the cosiest of them all - its wood-panelled rooms and leather armchairs make it a good bad weather destination (opening at 12pm when little of the lift system is running). If you can be bothered to leave the comfort of your seat you can entertain yourself with a game of pool. And if you fancy a snack a sandwich, crisps and chocolate meal combo is available - every whim catered for!

la taverne

méribel centre & mussilon après-ski & nightlife

bars
1 le saint amour
2 le poste de secours
3 le pub/scott's
4 bar le 's'
5 jack's
6 barometre
7 la taverne
8 fix
9 cactus café
nightclubs
10 le loft
11 dick's tea-bar
route de l'agentia
route du plateau
tremplin
la chaudanne
parc olympique
olympe
rhodos 1
burgin 1
tougnète
stade
roc de fer
plan de l'homme
100m
50m
0
a
b
c
d
e
f
1
2
3
4
n
s
copyright qanuk 2004

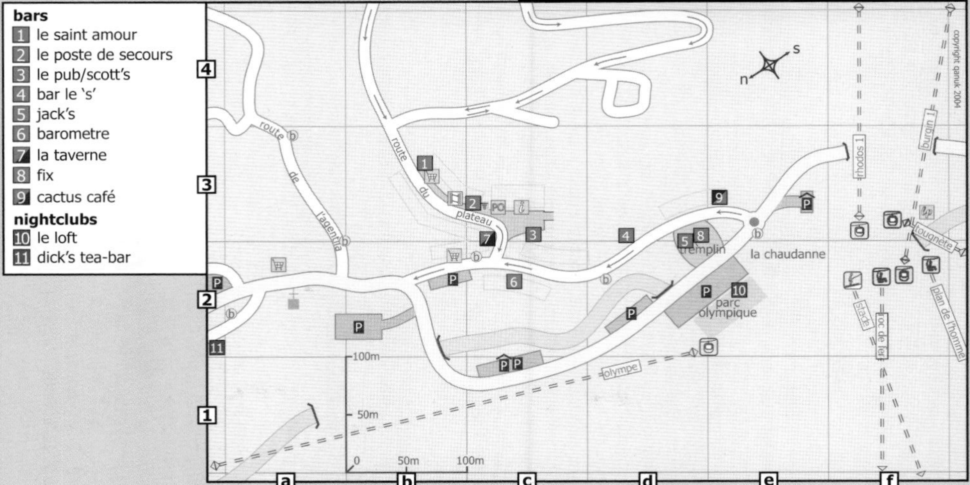

Music, food, Guinness... and the closest you'll get to an English pub - with dark wood and a hard-to-get-to bar. Showing chameleon tendencies La Taverne is something of an all-day venue. And it knows its (hungover) market well - opening early to serve a decent range of coffee to those missing their daily dose of Starbucks and hot baguettes (9:30am-11am) to soak up the excesses of the night before. Burgers and sandwiches are available upstairs (12pm-1am), while the downstairs restaurant opens in the evening for reasonably good classic French dining until 10:30pm, after which time it switches allegiance to Spain and serves tapas until 1am. With more happy hours than not, live music daily, live sporting events shown on a big screen and 10 internet terminals you may find you go nowhere else during your stay.

cactus café

A popular spot for lunch and après, partly because it is the first place you reach from the bottom of the pistes at La Chaudanne and partly because the food is inexpensive and neither pizza nor Savoyarde. Burgers and brasserie style meals are served during the day and Tex-Mex at night. Those just wanting to lounge around with a hot chocolate can set up home on one of the sofas, though the air can be a little smoky and steamy especially when live sport is being shown. With a generous 2 happy hours - 5pm-6pm and 10:30pm-11.30pm - and a range of flavoured tequila (including a fiesta-hot chilli version) - you are unlikely to leave sober.

le pub

The largest venue in town - though for some proof that size isn't everything - Le Pub on the main square is also the main host in town for the Alpine band scene. If your evening's mission is to find something strong, Le Pub can also provide that from its range of luridly coloured and interestingly flavoured vodkas (such as malteser) - or whatever is on special promotion. The time capsule entrance may make it look like the Pub takes itself a little too seriously, but actually it's just an effort to keep the raucous fun indoors.

le poste de secours

Part of the new wave of bars sweeping the Alps - in a former life this venue (known then as the Capricorn) was a favourite with seasonnaries. A recent revamp means it is now the hot hangout for Méribel's beautiful people - but as it so often the case stylish equals pricey.

98

But just pretend that you're in London and you won't blink twice at the cost of the very drinkable cocktails - and the non-London and very pleasant table service should help ease the pain. Prices aside, the modern interior, chic furnishings and cool music have made this a deservedly popular venue with all.

bar le 's'

For those torn between feeding the stomach and drowning the the liver, Bar Le 'S' on Route de la Montée complements its drinks menu with a tasty selection of tapas, French style. Though the bar is Australian run and Australian natured - the giveaway is the surf board outside - it has gained a following amongst the locals. What bigger compliment could you ask for?

scott's bar

Though Scott's shares its location with Le Pub, it is a decidedly more laid-back venue, where the emphasis is on cocktails and chat rather than pints and pulling. While it doesn't quite achieve the same level of chicness as the nearby Poste it is more affordable and snacks are available 4pm-9pm. Live music can be enjoyed from the comfort of one of the sofas.

dick's tea-bar

Though Dick's opens at 9pm, it is the late night venue of choice for the majority of the seasonnaire population and party-going holiday-makers. Its dark corners are perfect for hiding any sun-burned English complexion and its numerous theme nights (from school uniform parties to mardi gras fests) are a good way to break the ice. Entrance is free before 11pm and, dangerously, cocktails are 2 for 1 before midnight. And if you are a bit precious you can reserve a table in the 'VIP' section, where your every whim will be catered for - within reason.

le loft

Le Loft in the Parc Olympique is *plus chic* in style, *plus français* in clientele and p*lus grande* than Dick's. Something of club of 2 halves, the large dancefloor can accommodate most moves while the bar area provides a home for the more reserved. Its more cosmopolitan mix and less mainstream music not only make it a choice for the more discerning, but its central location means there is somewhere for the energetically challenged who don't fancy the walk down to (and back up from) Dick's.

If you stay in the suburbs, you'll find enough facilities to get you started without having to trudge down to the Centre. **le rond-point** is the most self-sufficient area - with its own ESF office, lift pass office, kindergarten, long-term covered parking, and a fair share of shops and hotels. It is also home to the best après spot on the mountain - the aptly named Rond-Point (➥ saulire). **belvédère** is something of a Club Med empire - 2 of the 3 Méribel-based Club Med hotels are found here - and at the far end you will find a gated enclave of huge, privately owned chalets. If your are led by your stomach, a stay in **morel** could suit you down to the ground - here you will find 2 of the best restaurants in the valley. And if you have your own plane the Altiport has to be the obvious choice.

<< eating out >>

Though none of the valley's restaurants are of world renown, Les Enfants Terribles is the most deserving. An intimate and friendly place, the central fireplace and candlelit surrounds make it cosy and the champagne cocktails will add an extra glow to your cheeks. Only open for dinner you can feast on the best French cuisine has to offer - foie gras, escargots and daily fish or meat specialities. As it is popular with both locals and visitors don't even think about going without a reservation.

The other French get-away in the suburbs, the speciality at Chez Kiki is charcoal grilled meat - so make sure your date is not a vegetarian. With its charmingly rustic appearance it is the Méribel's most authentic eaterie. The same building houses a cellar bar of the same name - which since the demise of El Poncho's is the only drinking hole this high up - and which provides a welcome change from the more English-geared places in the Centre.

Being the only non-hotel restaurant in walking distance of the accommodation around Le Rond-Point, Le Cro Magnon aims to be somewhere to eat for all men. Food ranges from Savoyarde specialities, pizza, pasta, fish and meat dishes - and is good in all categories. On most nights you need to book.

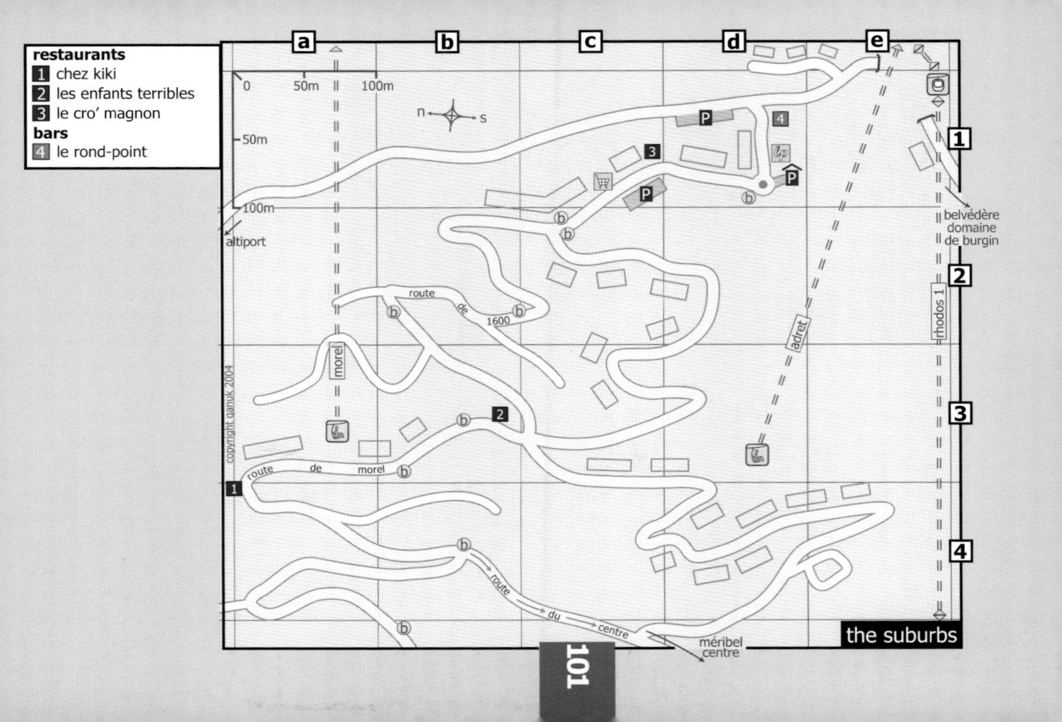

restaurants
1 chez kiki
2 les enfants terribles
3 le cro' magnon
bars
4 le rond-point
a
b
c
d
e
1
2
3
4
0
50m
100m
n
s
altiport
belvédère domaine de burgin
route de 1600
route de morel
route du centre
morel
adret
rhodos 1
méribel centre
copyright ganuk 2004
the suburbs

Despite its tiny size, Les Allues is the capital of the valley. A small and picturesque village it is similar to Courchevel's Le Praz in appearance and charm and is also where you find the perennial population - a mix of French and English residents. At 1100m, it is the lowest of the Méribel villages to cater for winter visitors - and since the construction of the Olympe gondola from Brides-les-Bains (which stops at a mid-station on the edge of the village), it has become a very viable option for those wanting alpine charm without the alpine crowds. The bulk of accommodation is found in privately-run chalets - or its 1 hotel - and during good seasons or the days after a decent snowfall you can ski back to the village along a piste from the Tougnète side of the valley. Though it is more peaceful than the Centre, Les Allues is home to one of the most popular night-time venues in the valley and has enough restaurants to stop you from going hungry. And though it is small it is perfectly formed, with a post office (open 2pm-5pm) a church, a library, a museum, a newsagent, a small but good supermarket (selling fruit, veg, fresh bread and cheese 8am-12pm, 4:30pm-7pm) and an English-run ski rental shop (Ski Higher).

<< eating out >>

One of the 2 Savoyarde options in Les Allues, La Chaumière on the valley road is a favourite with locals and visitors alike so reservations are essential. Food follows Savoyarde lines, and you can choose from a series of set menus. A cosy little place with a warming log fire, the décor is as typical to the region as the food, and the service is the most French that you will find.

Without doubt the English run Tsaretta is the liveliest venue in Les Allues - frequented by fun-lovers from all round the valley who make good use of the free shuttle provided. Though the restaurant on the first floor serves decent food, most people go there to drink and have a good time - and as you can have pizza and bar snacks downstairs who needs to make the effort to climb all those stairs. Theme nights are a regular occurence, as is live DJing - with tunes mixed by a local Englishman. You're guaranteed to sing along.

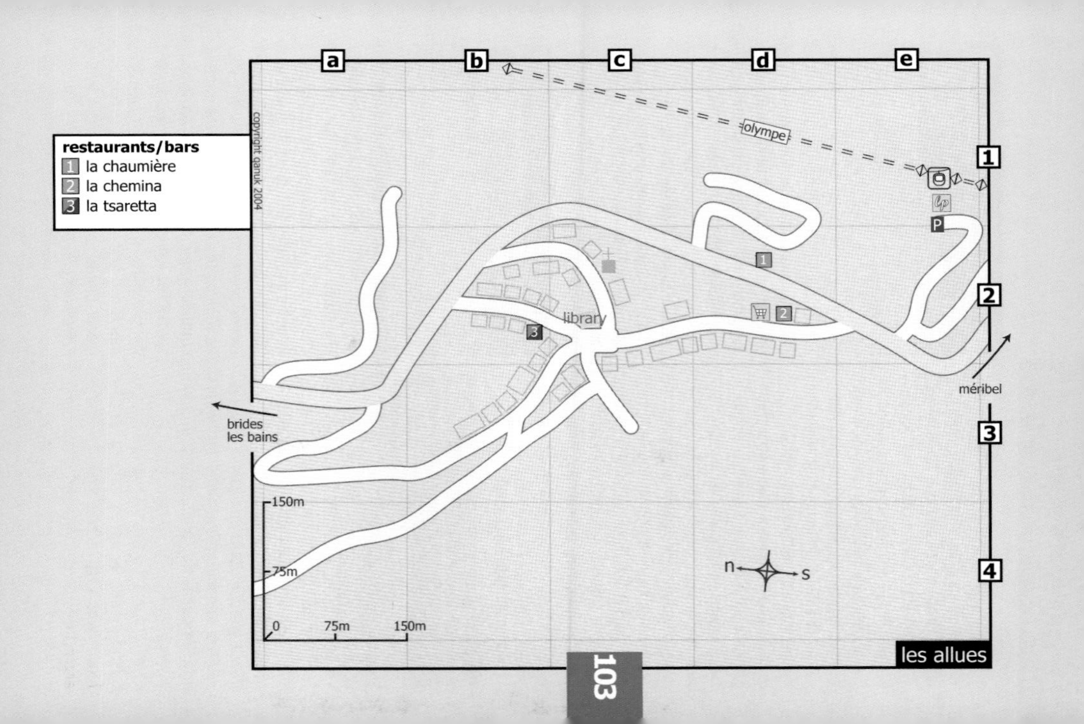

restaurants/bars
1 la chaumière
2 la chemina
3 la tsaretta
copyright qanuk 2004
a
b
c
d
e
1
2
3
4
olympe
library
méribel
brides
les bains
150m
75m
0
n
s
les allues

Méribel Village is the oldest village in the valley and lies about 1km from Centre, on the road to La Tania and Courchevel. Though some of the original buildings remain, these are now overshadowed by the fairly pretty MGM Les Fermes Village development. The infrastructure of the village is just big enough to survive on - in addition to 2 restaurants and an excellent bakery (from where you can get take-away pizza), there is a small supermarket, a lift pass office and a well-stocked ski rental shop - so you never need leave its friendly confines other than to ski. That is easy to as it is linked to the slopes around the Altiport by the Golf chairlift (on the way up) and the blue Lapin piste (on the way down).

<< eating out >>

Le Bo à Mil, tucked behind the Village's small chapel has been remarkably transformed from a stable to one of the cutest restaurants in the valley. The low, vaulted ceilings, stone walls and floors and wooden furniture create a snug atmosphere. The stone well in the courtyard and the relics hanging from the ceiling create as much interest as the food, which is traditional French - andincludes tender veal and spring lamb.

The younger sister of La Tania's Pub Le Ski Lodge, like its sibling the Lodge ticks the restaurant and the bar boxes. The ground floor restaurant is brightly furnished with Tuscany inspired murals - and serves pastas, pizzas and other Italian staples. The bar, run by a predominating English team, hosts live music (at least 3 times a week) and with its bright and airy look is more wine bar than pub - though when it's busy, the atmosphere is more pub than wine bar.

Not strictly in the Village, but about 1km down the road, and the place where you are most likely to be able to join in a chorus of Frère Jacques - it's not hard to imagine that this was used as a look-out post for the resistance in WW2. Don't worry about the slightly out-of-the-way location as the restaurant runs a minibus shuttle. All the usual Savoyarde specialities are on offer and you should be prepared to lose your English inhibitions and share a table with some fellow diners, and generally join in the French joie de vivre.

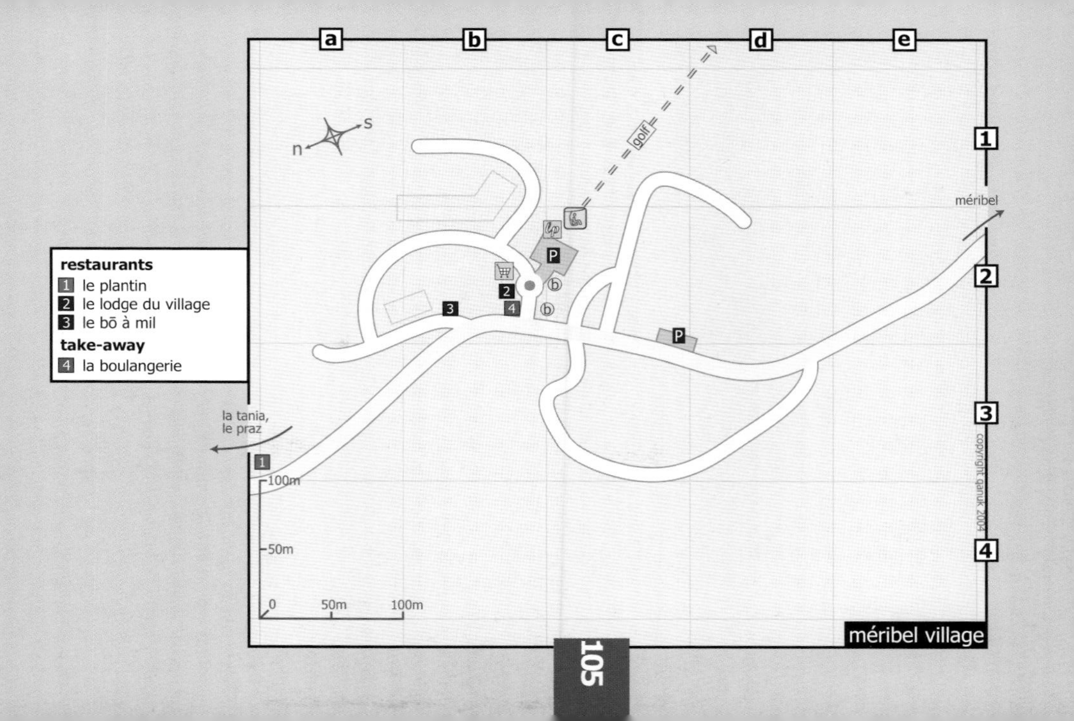
méribel village
restaurants
1 le plantin
2 le lodge du village
3 le bō à mil
take-away
4 la boulangerie
a
b
c
d
e
1
2
3
4
n
s
golf
méribel
la tania,
le praz
P
P
b
b
0
50m
100m
50m
100m
copyright qanuk 2004

The highest of the villages in the valley (lying between 1700m and 1800m) and a 10 minute bus ride from Centre. Mottaret is split into 2 main areas - Laitelet and Châtelet - and it exists solely for skiing purposes. No old-alpine charm here or generations of French mountain men. In fact the resort's advertising byline may as well be 'the very definition of convenience' such is the tidy neatness of its design - nearly all of the accommodation comes with the magic words "ski in/ski out" and the commerces and eateries are huddled in covered clusters at the bottom of the resort. The first accommodation appeared here in the early 1970s - and though they do not appear to have adhered to the same strict architectural guidelines as Méribel, they are not the high-rise monstrosities of some other purpose-built resort. The first impression of the resort as you approach it by road is of an endless ridgeline of apartment blocks, but don't be put off - there is more to Mottaret than meets the eye.

The original and older part of Laitelet is where you will find the most blocky accommodation and the original commerces, the tourist office, lift pass office and the ESF. A gondola lift (8am-7:30pm) links the commercial core at the bottom to the accommodation at the top (known as Le Hameau) - with a stop mid-way - where you will also find a scattering of restaurants, shops and bars. The alternative is a long and weary climb up over 400 metal steps - not advised in ski boots. A short walk across the *Front de Neige* takes you to the newer and more aesthetically pleasing Châtelet sitting on the Saulire side of the valley. Here too there is a cluster of commerces, eateries and drinkeries at the bottom of its accommodation. Though Mottaret wouldn't the top of the list for après-ski there are plenty of restaurants to keep your stomach happy and enough bars to remind your liver of its purpose. Just don't expect too many raucous nights, perhaps because the bulk of the holidaymakers who stay here are under the age of 16. The resort has just as good access as Méribel to the skiing in the Courchevel valley, and far better links to the Val Thorens valley, making it an ideal place to stay if you want to make full use of your 3 Vallées lift pass.

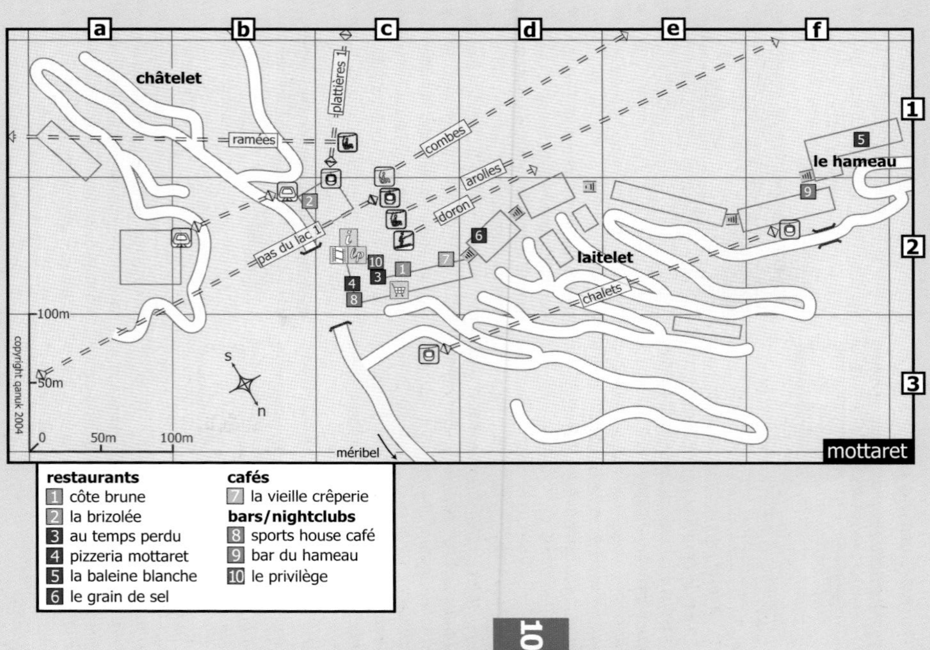
mottaret
a
b
c
d
e
f
1
2
3
châtelet
le hameau
laitelet
ramées
plattières 1
combes
arolles
doron
pas du lac 1
chalets
méribel
s
n
0
50m
100m
-50m
-100m
copyright qanuk 2004
restaurants
1 côte brune
2 la brizolée
3 au temps perdu
4 pizzeria mottaret
5 la baleine blanche
6 le grain de sel
cafés
7 la vieille crêperie
bars/nightclubs
8 sports house café
9 bar du hameau
10 le privilège

<< eating out >>

The Côte Brune's large sunny terrace and location at the bottom of Mottaret's pistes makes it a popular stop for lunch (12pm-3pm) and its friendly staff, laid-back atmosphere and *bon accueil* make it popular for evening dining. One of the first restaurants to open in Mottaret, it has a familial connection with Le Roc Tania at the top of the Col de la Loze, and food and service are of a similarly good standard. The cuisine is Savoyarde, although pizzas and the like are also available, while the wine list takes inspiration from further afield, with a number of good-quality Bordeaux grand crus. On sunny days, waffles and cold drinks are available from the stall outside.

108

Over towards Châtelet is Mottaret's most charming restaurant. With its wooden walls, rustic furniture and gingham checked curtains, you have the feeling of walking into a charmingly modernised mountain hut. The food too is local - all the Savoyarde specialities are available including a particularly excellent Pierre Chaude (like a table-top BBQ). The number of covers is restricted to 30 so it is good idea to book.

Though Proust was an unlikely visitor (not least because Au Temps Perdu has only been here since the 1970s) you won't be worried about the time you lose here. The style and food are Savoyarde, both for lunch and for dinner. The former can be taken on the huge terrace at the front - and if your stomach can't face a fondue there is a good selection of crêpes on the menu. Dinner is served in a cosy cellar room in the basement. And save room for dessert, as the home-made ice creams are to die for.

Though the name doesn't show much originality - pizza forms the base of many offerings on the menu and it is indeed in Mottaret - there is more to the Pizzeria Mottaret than meets the eye. Based over 2 levels, downstairs is where you will find the oven that cooks the pizzas and keeps the basement room ambiently warm. This is a direct contrast to the terrace at the front which, being surrounded by buildings, doesn't get much sun and is not somewhere for a lengthy lunch. Should you not want pizza there are plenty of other choices - from meat-based dishes to Savoyarde specialities - and should you decide not to stay you can take away your choice of pizza.

The names of the restaurants in Mottaret's Le Hameau area have something of an animal-theme. The Baleine Blanche is no exception and has the reputation as one of the best in the resort. Though the menu includes typical Savoyarde dishes, some come with an unusual twist, such as the pleasingly cheap and very tasty duck fondue - but fortunately you won't find the namesake animal (white whale) on the menu. Due to its popularity the restaurant runs 2 sittings for dinner.

More café than restaurant, La Vieille Crêperie is tucked away at the far end of the shopping complex, just before the the steps up to Laitelet's apartments. Housed in a small room, crêpes are very much the order of the day, though ice-cream sundaes come a close second - the menu is one that those with a sweet tooth will find hard to resist. There isn't a terrace, but the lack of one just makes this somewhere even more suitable for an inhospitable day when all you want is some comfort food.

and the rest

With such a prime position at the bottom of the slopes, Mottaret has more lunchtime venues than there are days in your skiing holiday. The obvious stops are the Côte Brune and Au Temps Perdu, though as they are obvious to most skiers on their descent to the resort they can be very busy. For a better chance of a seat try any of the smaller places found on the other side of the Mont Vallon hotel and along the gallery of commerces below Châtelet. Of these the British-frequented **le rastro** (t 0479 004151) is quiet enough for lunch - by night it becomes an altogther more lively animal, particularly on Tuesday nights. The **zig zag** (t 0479 004770) looks little more than a hut - and there is more seating inside than out - but the small kitchen can produce wonders. The plat du jour is normally a good place to start.

A journey down the Furet piste takes you past **le grain de sel** (t 0479

003082), a relatively new addition to the restaurant scene - lunch is typically omelettes and pasta while the evening menu includes delicacies such as foie gras and steak. Of the hotel restaurants the Mark Warner-run **tarentaise** is recommended.

Another of the animal offerings at Le Hameau is **la taverne du crocodile** (t 0479 004585) with another menu of Savoyarde staples. You will also find **le tysable** (t 0479 004342) in Le Hameau - the oldest restaurant at this end of the resort, it is a sweet little bistro and the haunt of one of the most charming patrons in the valley. It probably goes without saying that the food is Savoyarde.

Mottaret does take-away like nowhere else - even the sit-down restaurants are in on the act. **fast food** on the Front de Neige serves standard sandwiches and snacks 7:30am-5:30pm. **la chrismamara**, immediately next to the Sports House Café, is the last option for food before bedtime - it serves paninis, sanwiches, burgers, hot-dogs, chips and the ubiquitous kebab until late.

<< après-ski & nightlife >>

sports house café

0479 085684
8am-1:30am

Tucked away by the Pizzeria Mottaret and the kebab shop, the Sports House café is where the younger end of the population hang out - and some of its clientele should probably be asked for ID. Minimal in design and décor, the drinks menu is fuller, offering a range of liquid refreshment from hot chocolate to beer - and the bar has a Giraffe for those who've got a bit of a thirst on. Those who get bored of the company they go with can surf the internet, watch the game or play video games. Though on quiet nights it can feel a bit like a youth club that is no longer in fashion, when it is busy, the atmosphere is buzzing.

bar le hameau

0479 004646
8am-1am

The Bar at Le Hameau can come as something of a surprise - not least because there is nothing much outside to advertise it. Just make sure you notice where it is before you make the long trek to the bottom of the resort and the other drinking venues. Happy hour runs from 6-7pm (though not on cocktails) and you can stack up the beers whilst watching news and sport TV. The Bar is part of the

Domaine du Soleil complex, and you can take your drink to the room next door if you fancy a game of pool. Some nights are surprisingly busy, when the bar fills with seasonnaires and holiday-makers - presumably because nobody can be bothered with those stairs.

le privilège

Mottaret's only official nightclub, after the Sports House café closes at 1:30am, it's here or it's up the stairs to bed-fordshire. Located underneath the piste, for years the Privilège festered as a sub-snow dive, but a recent change of ownership has brought it a new lease of life - and a somewhere for Mottaret's seasonnaires to get to know each other a bit better. Entrance is €12 (though that also gets you a free drink) or groups of 5 people can pay €110 and get a free bottle of spirits. Theme nights are now a feature though on other nights it can be a bit of a lottery as to whether it's dead or heaving - and from the outside there are few clues as to which.

and the rest

The **down town bar** on the Front de Neige is a buzzy place that provides the first drink to a lot of skiers at the end of the day - it is a good place to catch the last of the rays and has 2 happy hours (4pm-6pm). A more civilised alternative can be found just across the snow, at the terrace bar in front of the Mont du Vallon hotel - or any of the restaurant terraces in the same area.

When the lifts are closed because of too little or - more frustratingly - too much snow, there a few things to keep you occupied. The Méribel tourist office publishes a weekly pamphlet (*"les coups de coeur de la semaine"* or 'highlights of the week'), a 7 day schedule in English and French which details the events taking place in the resort each week.

airborne

Ski Vol (t 0479 084172) run **air balloon** flights from ½ to 1 hour over the valley (weather permitting - wear plenty of clothes as it doesn't get any warmer up there. **aeroplane** flights from the Altiport over the valley, the 3 Vallées and the Mont Blanc massif can be booked through Méribel-Air (t 0479 011022). There are also 3 **parapenting** schools: Tandom Top (t 0479 004567), Ski Sensations Flights (t 0608741829) or Fly (t 0671 902195) - the launching point for most take-offs is the sunny plateau at Col de la Loze on the Saulire side.

olympic glory

If you haven't had enough exercise the best memento of the 1992 Winter Olympics at Albertville is the huge **parc olympique** at La Chaudanne. Whilst not as aesthetically pleasing as the rest of the village (the building code seems to have been largely ignored), it does house impressive sports facilities. The **climbing wall** (t 0479 003038, 9am-9pm) can be used by the experienced whenever and the Bureau des Guides run beginner's courses Tuesdays and Thursdays 6pm-8pm, though the guides can be a little invisible and embrace the French concept of a long lunch. The 25m **indoor swimming pool** (t 0479 005821) is open daily (2pm-7:15pm) and Tuesday and Thursday evenings until 9:15pm - under 5s swim for free, adults for €5, kids for €3. The **ice rink** (t 0479 005821) is open to the public daily (2pm-7:30pm) and Tuesday and Thursday nights until 9:30pm. Entrance is €5 and lessons and skates are available. The ice rink is also host to a programme of ice hockey matches throughout the season where you can marvel at their ability to stay standing on the ice and hit a small black pudding.

bad weather options

There are 2 **cinemas** in the valley - 1 in Mottaret (t 0479 004235) and 1 in Méribel (t 0479 086502, i cinealpes.fr). Look for films marked VOST (*Version Originale*) for English language films. There are normally 2 screenings each day (5:30pm and 9pm) and an extra one at 2:30pm in bad weather. Most films shown are mainstream releases. The Parc Olympique has a 10-pin **bowling alley** (t 0479 003644) but there are only 6 lanes (open daily 2pm-2am and from 11am on bad weather days) so it's best to book. Those who don't like the look of the shoes that must be worn can entertain themselves at the bar or the pool tables and in front of a big TV screen on which major sporting events are broadcast.

inner calm

If your muscles are too stiff to move, Pamper Off Piste (t 0479 006256/ 0617608902, i pamperoffpiste.com) offers a mobile **massage** service (daily 8am-8pm). The Club Med spa in the Aspen Park hotel at Le Rond-Point (t 0479 005177) offers an extensive range of beauty and health treatments - bookings are essential - as does Le Ludicur Centre (t 0479 088908, Mondays-Saturdays 9:30am-7:30pm) in the hotel Chaudanne, which also has a hairdresser. You may find yourself praying for a full week of bad weather. You can also use the hotel's leisure facilities (which include a sauna and jacuzzi). And those missing the motivating encouragment of their aerobics teacher can go to the fitness classes held at Les Sources du Bien-Etre fitness centre (t 0479 013200)in Méribel Village - classes include 'tums & waists', 'stretching' and 'relaxing' and are held in the mornings and late afternoons, and you can relax after in the sauna, and turkish bath.

education

You can visit the valley's **snow-making centre** to see how the artificial stuff is made - a talk is given in French so take your dictionary. You can also take a trip on a snowcat (Mondays-Fridays) to see how it is then groomed. Both activities are very popular so you need to book well in advance - through the Méribel-Alpina lift office at La Chaudanne.

Les Allues has a small **museum** (open Tuesdays and Thursdays 2pm-6.30pm) in the Bonnevie House, which has a permanent exhibition of the valley's history and traditions. Further afield (in Moûtiers) you can pay a visit to one of the local **cheesemakers** (t 0479 240365) and see how the main ingredient in your fondue gets made.

flex your credit

The **casino** in Brides-Les-Bains (t 0479 552307) is open 7 days a week 2pm-late) and will gladly relieve you of your money in its slot machines or at the black jack tables - and if you lose it all you can take solace in the on-site restaurant, bar or night club.

shopaholics will have to content themselves with sports equipment or clothes. The streets of Centre are lined with brands you will recognise - Fat Face, White Stuff and O'Neill - all of which sell the same stuff that you can find back home. And there is a bi-weekly market on the street, selling bargain price fleeces and local produce.

The 3 Vallées among the best areas to go skiing as a family. Méribel is one of the 57 French resorts to have been awarded the P'tit Montagnards status - which indicates that the resort is suitable for families and children on the basis of 9 criteria. Because of the resort's popularity with families, it is essential to book what you need - nurseries, ski lessons for your children - before you arrive.

tour operators

simply ski run a chalet-based nanny service during the day (as long as you reserve the whole chalet). The nanny can look after up to 3 children at any one time (aged 6 months-8 years). **mériski** offers a nanny service during the day for children aged 6 years and under. Children are either whisked off to their resort-based crèche at 8:30am or you can arrange for a nanny to look after them in the chalet where you are staying. Children aged 6-12 can attend the Mérikids club. A nanny can also be booked for evening babysitting - for an extra charge. **mark warner** offers childcare in its chalet-hotel in Mottaret for children aged 4 months-12 years. Extra babysitting services can be arranged and a member of the childcare team keeps an evening watch (7:30pm-11pm) so you can enjoy your own après. The British-run nanny service **snow kidz** (t 0870 402 8888, i snow kidz.com) will arrange childcare at your chalet - all nannies are British and have the relevant qualifications. The service is available Sundays-Fridays 9am-5pm, and you can also arrange evening babysitting through them. Nannies work to the ratio of 1:2 for children under 2 years and 1:3 for children over 3 years.

in-resort

Les P'tits Loups is an ESF-run **kindergarten** for children aged 3-5 years. Based at Le Rond-Point (t 0479 086060), La Chaudanne (t 0479 086690) and Mottaret (t 0479 003666) and open 9am-5pm children can enjoy the private snow-covered playground and learn how to use the specially designed ski lifts. For younger children the **les saturnins** (t 0479 086690) day nursery in the Olympic Centre takes children aged 18months-3 years. Also associated with the ESF, ski lessons are offered to those children who are ready to ski. Care is available on a half day or full day basis, with or without lunch.

114

The tourist office, your hotel or apartment manager can put you in touch with qualified private **babysitters** who provide child care services at any time of the day or night - and there are plenty of willing seasonnaires available as ad hoc babysitters. **kids etcetera** (t 0479 007139/0622 626903 (mobile), i kidsetc.co.uk) is a well established and trusted organisation run by a Brit. All the nannies have the necessary childcare qualifications, and they are available to look after children of all ages on a private or playgroup basis, during the day or evening.

The ESF runs ski **lessons** for children of all levels of ability (9:30am-12:15pm, 2:30pm-4:45pm) betwee 5-13 years. During the school holidays in February English-speaking children are put in the same groups. The ESF also run a slalom course during the school holidays for children aged 10 and over, while those over 14 can join the freeride/freestyle course which gives an introduction to off-piste/new school skiing. They also run boarding lessons for children aged 8 and over. While the other schools only run lessons for children during the school holidays, Ski Academy's children's programme runs for the entire season. Children need a **lift pass** to attend ski lessons or the ski-based kindergartens - even if they qualify for the free pass. You can save money by buying a children's lift passes as part of a ski school package.

Entertainment for children doesn't stop once the lifts close. The ESF organises night-time **snowshoe** excursions for children aged 6-12 years (or book direct on t 0660 117568) as well as weekly **torchlit** descents. The resort also organises activities for children around the festive periods of Christmas, Mardi Gras and Easter.

If you forget to pack everything that you need you can rent push chairs, high chairs and folding cots from Une Souris Verte (t 0479 011954) on Route de la Chaudanne - they also sell children's clothes and accessories.

before you go

Before you decide what kind of job you want you need to decide what kind of season you want - a job as a rep will be better paid but you have more responsibility, while a job as a chalet host means fixed hours, but once you know the routine, more time to make the most of resort life. Most of the UK ski companies recruit seasonal workers - interviewing normally starts in May, though there may still be vacancies as late as December. Either contact the companies directly (not forgetting smaller or overseas based ones) or go through a recruitment website such as **findaskijob.com**, **snowsportrecruitment.com** or **natives** (i natives.co.uk) - the last has a comprehensive database of available jobs as well as a lot of useful information on everything about "doing a season". It's a competitive market for jobs and while it is not essential, speaking reasonable French will help. If you haven't got a job by October, it's worth going to the Ski Show in London - some tour operators have a stall there as does Natives. If you haven't got a job by the start of the season, it can be worth heading out to the resort (if you can support yourself for a bit). Some of the less glamourous jobs may still be available and you will also get known - so when there is the inevitable fall-out of recruits due to unsuitability, New Year flu and mid-season blues, you can step into the role. Jobs constantly become available throughout the season - the ski market is very transient. Once employed most companies organise your work permit, your travel to and from the resort, accommodation, lift pass and equipment rental. Most seasonnaire jobs come with a shared room as part of the package. If you don't get accommodation with your job - or if you aren't planning on having a job - you would be well advised to find some digs before you head out. The accommodation situation in the Méribel valley is not as bad as over in Courchevel and in general a group of 4 or more people should be able to find somewhere that won't break the bank. **planet subzero** (i planetsubzero.com) has a 3-bedroom apartment in the centre of Méribel, which sleeps 6/7 people - you can reserve it for anything from 1 month to the whole season. Single or double apartments are a little harder to come by, and accordingly can be pretty pricey. And if you'd rather live with the locals, Les Allues is the best bet - with a well-established, long-term population, half French, half English.

once you're there

With so many English tour operators, the seasonnaire community is bound to be a little cliquey - but in a one-big-happy-family way. A fair number of seasonnaires go to Méribel for the après rather than the skiing - and if that's what you want it's certainly on offer. With the demise of the Capricorn which **hangout** is 'the' hangout is a bit of a moveable feast. That said, Tsaretta in Les Allues and the Lodge du Village in the Village are popular - in the latter you'll get a discount off their menu if you go in with a group of clients. Méribel has a reputation for being good to its seasonnaires - possibly because a number of the establishments are English owned or English run. Many of the bars will charge you happy hour prices even when it's not - and it's happy hour all day, all season for seasonnaires at **le rond-point**. In the Centre, €25 and a photo gets you a season ticket for Dick's - though you may be lucky enough to scoop one of the free tickets they hand out from time to time. Some shops will give you up to a 15% discount on stock.

If you have good intentions to learn something while you're there - and capitalise on it early on before they disappear into a haze of vodka shooters - some of the ski schools will sell you lessons at a discount and you can also get language lessons. For bookworms, membership of the library in Les Allues (open 3pm-7:30pm Mondays, Wednesdays and Fridays) is a bargain €8 for the season. If you need a bit of cooking practice whilst there, Jerry Mant runs classes in chalet Bartavelle (t 0479 081955, chalet-bartavelle-meribel.co.uk)

Calls home are expensive from an English **mobile**, so it could be worth investing in a French SIM card (try the phone shop in the Hyper Champion in Moûtiers - generally about £30 (of which £15 is call credit) and calls made within and out of France will be cheaper and you won't pay to receive calls from the UK. Check that your phone is 'unlocked' (so you can insert a foreign SIM card into it) before you leave the UK. You then pay as you go as you would in the UK. Top up cards are available from the newsagents in Centre. For **internet** access the Cybar in the basement of La Taverne has 10 terminals. The tourist office have 2 card-operated machines and will also let you plug in your own laptop for €2 per 10 minutes. If you have your own PC and want to get on-line, sign up to free.fr for free access (you only pay for a local call charge) or try wanadoo.fr. For daily information about the resort, Europe 2 (97.9 and 98.9FM) becomes Radio Méribel in the morning and evening and broadcasts what's going on in and around the area, including lift, piste and weather reports and a 'What's On Today' in English from around 7:30am, and English news at 8:30am. The Méribel Times is a local on-line publication - though editions can be a little irregular. Something much more reliable is the seasonnaire **grapevine**. Do something outrageous, and your 'friends' across town will likely know all about it before you even remember it yourself.

the a-z

tour operators

A list of the English based tour operators offering a range of accommodation in the Méribel valley. Though many of them offer a variety of different ways to take a skiing holiday they have been categorised according to their main strength.

mainstream

airtours t 0870 238 7777,
i mytravel.com
club med t 0700 2582 932,
i clubmed.co.uk
crystal t 0870 405 5047,
i crystalski.co.uk
first choice t 0870 850 3999,
i fcski.co.uk
french life ski t 0870 197 6692,
i frenchlifeski.co.uk
inghams t 020 8780 4433,
i inghams.co.uk
leisure direction t 020 8324 4042,
i leisuredirection.co.uk
lotus supertravel t 020 7295 1650,
i supertravel.co.uk
mark warner t 0870 770 4227,
i markwarner.co.uk
neilson t 0870 333 3356,
i neilson.co.uk
thomson t 0870 606 1470,
i thomson-ski.co.uk

ski-specific

on the piste travel t 01625 503 111,
i onthepiste.co.uk
silver ski t 01622 735 544,
i silverski.co.uk
simply ski t 0208 541 2209,
i simplytravel.co.uk
ski activity t 01738 840 888,
i skiactivity.co.uk
ski amis t 020 7692 0850, i skiamis.com
ski beat t 01243 780 405,
i skibeat.co.uk
ski club of great britain t 020 8410 2022, i skiclub.co.uk
ski independence t 0870 600 1462,
i ski-independence.co.uk
ski olympic t 01302 328 820,
i skiolympic.co.uk
ski world t 08702 416723,
i skiworld.ltd.uk
snowline t 0208 870 4807,
i snowline.co.uk

resort-specific & independents

absolute ski t 01788 822100,
i absoluteski.com
accommodation in the alps t 0870 136 4311, i accommodationinthealps.co.uk
alp leisure t 0479 005942,
i alpleisure.com
alpine action t 01273 597940, i alpine-action.co.uk
alpine infusion t 01844 344955,
i alpineinfusion.com
alps à la carte t 01494 730705,
i alpsalacarte.com
bonne neige t 01270 256966, i bonne-neige-ski.com
chalet bartavelle t 0479 081955,
i chalet-bartavelle-meribel.co.uk (Le Cruet)
chalet chanticleer t 07050 200612,
i skimoments.com (Belvédère)
chalet chardon bleu t 0479 241593,
i ski-chardonbleu.com (Mottaret)
chalet du guide t 01223 892731,

i chaletduguide.com (Méribel Village)
chalet génépi t 01932 349 585,
i genepi.net (Belvédère)
chalet le yéti t 0207 351 2734,
i meribelchalet.com
cooltip mountain holidays t 01964 563 563, i cooltip.com
edel ski t 0494 547256,
i edelski.com (Mussillon)
mériski t 01285 648518, i meriski.co.uk
purple ski t 01494 488633,
i purpleski.co.uk
ski basics t 01225 444 143,
i skibasics.co.uk
ski blanc t 0208 502 9082,
i skiblanc.co.uk
ski bon t 0208 668 8223, i skibon.com
ski cuisine t 01702 589 543,
i skicuisine.co.uk
ski out of the blue t 01245 248171,
i skiblue.co.uk
snow trip t 0845 200 6794,
i snowtrip.co.uk
the oxford ski company t 01451 810300,
i oxfordski.com
very belle ski t 07967 052 382,
i verybelleski.com

luxury

alp leisure t 0479 005942,
i alpleisure.com
descent t 0207 384 3854,
i descent.co.uk
elegant resorts t 01244 897 333,
i elegantresorts.co.uk
kaluma travel t 0870 4428044,
i kalumatravel.co.uk
VIP t 0208 875 1957, i vip-chalets.com

self-catering & budget

ams t 01743 340623, i amsrentals.com
interhome t 020 8891 1294,
i interhome.co.uk
into mountains i intomountains.com
skiholidays4less t 01724 290660,
i french-freedom.co.uk

self-drive

drive alive t 0114 292 2971, i drive-alive.com
erna low t 0207 584 2841,
i ernalow.co.uk
eurotunnel motoring holidays t 0870 333 2001, i eurotunnel.com

tailor-made & weekends

made to measure holidays t 0124 353 3333, i madetomeasureholidays.com
momentum ski t 0207 371 9111,
i momentum.uk.com
ski weekend t 0870 060 0615,
i skiweekend.com
white roc ski weekends t 0207 792 1188, i whiteroc.co.uk

If you run a ski company that offers holidays to Méribel but are not listed here, let us know and we'll include you in the next edition of this guide.

directory

listings

All 04 or 06 numbers need the French international prefix (0033) if dialled from the UK. 08 numbers can only be dialled within France.

transport

air

bmibaby t 0870 264 2229,
i bmibaby.com
british airways t 0870 850 9850,
i ba.com
easyjet t 0870 600 0000,
i easyjet.co.uk
ryanair i ryanair.co.uk
swiss t 0845 601 0956, i swiss.com
chambéry t 0479 544966, i aeroport-chambery.com
geneva t 0041 22 717 7111, i gva.ch
grenoble t 0476 654848,
i grenoble.aeroport.fr
lyon t 0826 800826, i lyon.aeroport.fr
st. etienne t 0477 557171, i saint-etienne.aeroport.fr

car hire

alamo i alamo.com
avis i avis.com (Moûtiers) t 0479 240793
easycar t 0906 333 3333
i easycar.com
europcar i europcar.com (Méribel t 0479 040420)
hertz t 0870 844 8844 i hertz.co.uk (Méribel t 0479 004527/5960/086329)

coach travel

eurolines t 08705 143219,
i nationalexpress.com
ski méribel t 0208 668 8223,
i skimeribel.co.uk

cross-channel

eurotunnel t 0870 535 3535,
i eurotunnel.com
norfolkline t 01304 218400,
i norfolkline.com
speedferries t 01304 203000
i speedferries.com

driving

general - carry a valid driver's licence, proof of ownership, your insurance certificate and an emergency triangle.
petrol - there is 1 petrol station (not 24 hr) on the main road up in the valley though it is better to fill up in Moûtiers, as higher altitude means higher prices.
signs & rules - motorways in France have blue signs. Most operate a péage (toll) system. You must wear a seatbelt in the front and back of a car. Children under 12 must sit in the back and babies and young children must be placed in special baby/young child seats.
speed limits - in built-up areas the speed limit is 50km/h (unless indicated). The limit is 90km/h on all other roads, 110km/h on toll-free motorways and 130km/h on toll motorways. Foreign drivers are given spot fines for speeding.
traffic info - (recorded) t 0826 022022

helicopter

(SAF) t 0479 080091, i saf-helico.com

international train

raileurope t 0870 584 8848
i raileurope.co.uk
eurostar t 0870 518 6186
i eurostar.com
TGV i tgv.com

local train

SNCF t 0892 353535, 0479 005328 (Méribel), i ter-sncf.com/rhone-alpes

private bus

alp line t 0677 865282, i alp-line.com
alpine cab i alpinecab.com.
ats t 0709 209 7392, i a-t-s.net
mountain transfers t 07889 942786, i mountaintransfers.com
three vallée transfers t 01782 644 420, i 3vt.co.uk

public bus

méribus t 0479 085366
satobus alpes t 0472 359496, i satobus-alps.com
touriscar t 0450 436002, i alpski-bus.com
transavoie t 0479 085490, i altibus.com
moûtiers bus station t 0479 242446

health & safety

accidents

If you have an accident on the slopes, you will be taken to the nearest doctor unless you specify a particular one. To confirm you can pay for treatment you will need a credit card and your insurance details. At some point, contact your insurance company to check whether they want to arrange your transport home - and ask your doctor for a medical certificate confirming you are fit to travel. If you see an accident on the slopes, tell the nearest rescue centre, usually found at the top or bottom of lifts.

doctors

The main medical centre is at the Parc Olympique (t 0479 086041, 9:30am-7pm), where there are doctors and a dentist and a 24 hour telephone helpline. There is also a medical practice in 1600 (t 0479 086540) and 1 in Mottaret (t 0479 004088). The nearest hospital is in Moûtiers (t 0479 096060) and the nearest casualty is in Albertville.

emergency numbers

ambulance t 0479 552867
emergencies (including fire) t 18 (from a land line), t 112 (from a mobile)
emergency medical care (SAMU) t 15
police (gendarmerie) t 17 or t 0479 086017
police municipale t 0479 005892 (weekdays 10am-12:30pm, 3:30pm-7pm)
s.a.f. helicoptérès t 0479 080091

health

An E111 form (available from any UK post office) entitles you to treatment under the French health system. While you have to pay for your treatment when you receive it, you can then get a refund for up to 70% of medical expenses - as long as you keep all your receipts.

insurance

It is essential to have personal insurance covering wintersports and the cost of any ambulances, helicopter rescue and emergency repatriation - all these services are very expensive. Insurance policies differ greatly - some exclude off-piste skiing or cover it only if you are with a guide, so you need to check the terms and conditions carefully.

pharmacies

There is one in Centre (Rue de Montée, t 0479 086359), open 8:30am-1pm, 2:30pm-7:15pm. In Mottaret there is one in the main area of shops at the bottom of Laitelet (t 0479 004370).

physiotherapists

Christophe Lavoué in the Parc Olympique (t 0479 003143), Cyrille Alda in 1600 (t 0622 158435) or Laure Mandry and Claude Bohé-Gérard in Les Allues (t 0479 010828).

safety on the mountain

avalanche danger - the risk of avalanche is graded from 1 to 5.
1 & 2. (yellow) low risk.
3 & 4. (checked yellow and black) moderate risk, caution advised when skiing off-piste
5. (black) high risk, off-piste skiing strongly discouraged.
The risk is displayed on a flag at the main lift stations, but if you are in any doubt about where it is safe to ski, ask the advice of the lift operators.

food & drink - a skiing holiday is not the time to start a diet. Your body expends energy keeping warm and exercising so it's a good idea to eat a decent breakfast, and carry some chocolate or sweets with you. The body dehydrates more quickly at altitude and whilst exercising. You need to drink a lot (of water) each day to replace the moisture you lose.

rules of conduct - the International Ski Federation publishes conduct rules for all skiers and boarders:
1. respect - do not endanger or prejudice others.
2. control - ski in control, adapting speed and manner to ability, the conditions and the traffic.
3. choice of route - the uphill skier must choose his route so he does not endanger skiers ahead.
4. overtaking - allowed above or below, right or left, but leave enough room for the overtaken skier.
5. entering & starting a run - look up and down the piste when doing so.
6. stopping on the piste - avoid stopping in narrow places or where visibility is restricted.
7. climbing - keep to the side of the piste when climbing up or down.
8. signs & markings - respect these.
9. assistance - every skier must assist at accidents.
10. identification - all involved in an accident (including witnesses) must exchange details.

snow & avalanche information

t 0892 681020

weather

Get daily updates t 0892 680273 (French) or online at i meteo.fr.

what to wear

Several, thin layers are better than one thick piece. Avoid cotton, which keeps moisture next to the body, so cooling it down. A windproof and waterproof material (such as Goretex) is best for outer layers. A hat is essential to keep you warm and protect the scalp from sunburn as are gloves to keep hands warm. Sunglasses or goggles are essential. Wrap-arounds are a good choice and lenses should be shatter-proof and give 100% protection from UVA and UVB rays. Poor eye protection can lead to snowblindness, which makes the eyes water and feel painful and gritty. Treat by resting eyes in a darkened room, and applying cold compresses. You should wear UVA and UVB sun protection with a high factor (SPF) at all times, even if overcast and cloudy. The sun is more intense at higher altitude, so you should re-apply regularly (particularly after falling or sweating). Don't forget to cover your ear lobes and the underside of the nose.

resort survival

banks & atms

In Centre there are 3 banks - Banque de Savoie, Banque Populaire and Crédit Agricole all of which have ATMs, as does the post office (which also has a bureau du change).

In Mottaret there is an ATM (Crédit Agricole) only in Laitelet.

church services

The Catholic church of St. Martin in Les Allues holds daily services at 6pm, with a free shuttle from Méribel. There are several Protestant services during the week - detailed in the weekly newsletter.

internet/email

The Méribel tourist office has 2 terminals (which take phone cards) and will also let you connect your own laptop (€2 for 10 minutes). La Taverne has 10 terminals and Le Petit Rond-Point and the Cactus Café have terminals as well. The Mottaret tourist office has a phone-card operated terminal as well, or try the Sporthouse Café.

laundry & dry cleaning

The Laverie Pingouin'net at La Chaudanne is a self-service laundrette open daily 8:30am-9:30pm.

newspapers

Newspapers are available from the various *presses* at inflated prices.

parking

The valley has numerous charging and free car parks. Parking alongside the roads is allowed in designated areas - though this is mainly pay & display in the Centre. At weekends the car parks become very busy and make sure that no snow clearing activity is planned (signs indicate when and where) or your car will be removed. Also, when the spring melt starts make sure you are not parked under a "chute de neige" as your car may be slightly smaller when you come back.

passport photos

Both the tourist offices have passport photo booth, and there is also one at La Chaudanne.

post

There are 3 offices in the valley - 1 in each of Méribel Centre (which also has a bureau de change), Mottaret and Les Allues (which is only open in the afternoons).

radio

Radio Méribel 97.9 and 98.9FM (t 0479 085907) broadcasts English reports on the weather, snow conditions and resort life 7:30am-10am and 5pm-7pm.

shopping

Most shops open daily (except public holidays) 8:30am-12:30pm and 2:30pm-7pm (though some lunch for longer).
supermarkets - the largest supermaket is Casino in Mussillon (open daily, 8:30am-12:30pm, 3pm-7:30pm). Centre and each of Les Allues and the Village have their own small supermarket. Mottaret also has a Sherpa (open daily).
local produce - La Fromagerie in Galeire des Cimes is the place to head for delicious cheese, or you can wait for the weekly market where you will find stalls selling cured meats as well as the smelly stuff.

ski lockers

Meribel-Alpina runs a locker room at La Chaudanne (8:45am-5:45pm).

taxis

There are a number of taxi companies to choose from, including:
méritaxis t 0479 085822
taxiphone méribel t 0479 086510
taxiphone méribel/mottaret t 0479 004429
The tourist office can provide you with a fuller list

tourist offices

The main office is on the square in Méribel Centre (t 0479 086001, i meribel.net), daily 9am-7pm - you can also book accommodation and book ski school and transport reservations. The Mottaret office (t 0479 004234) is located at the bottom of the resort and has the same opening hours and similar information - though they will direct you to Méribel for some things.

websites

There are a number of Méribel websites, which give information of varying degrees of accuracy. The tourist office is very proud of their site, while one of the best independent sites (and the original) is merinet.com.

country survival

customs
As France is part of the EU, there are few restrictions on what UK visitors can take out for personal use.

electricity
220 volts/50hz ac. Appliances use a two-pin plug - adaptors are readily available from electrical stores or supermarkets.

language
English is widely spoken, though an attempt at French is appreciated in the locally-run places.

money
The currency is the Euro (€). €1 is equivalent to 100 centimes. Notes come in anything from €10 to €500. You can exchange money in all the banks and at the post office. In 2004, the average exchange rate for UK£1 = (approx) €1.6

public holidays
December 6 - St Nicholas Day
25 - Christmas Day
26 - St Stephen's day
January 1 - New Year's Day
March/April Good Friday, Easter Sunday & Monday

telephone
Public phones boxes are located throughout the resorts and accept coins or phonecards, which can be bought from the post office, tabacs, and train and petrol stations. All local and calls within Europe are cheaper 7pm-8am during the week and all day at the weekend. The international dialling code for France is 0033; the free international operator 12; the international directory information 1159; and national directory information 111. There are three mobile phone networks: Bouygues Telecom, France telecom/Orange and SFR.

time
France is always 1 hour ahead of England.

tipping
All food bills include a service charge, though it is common to make an addition for drinks or for noticeably good service.

water
Tap water is drinkable, except where there is an *eau non potable* sign.

glossary

a

arête - a sharp ridge.

avalanche - a rapid slide of snow down a slope.

avalanche transceiver - a device used when skiing off-piste, which can both emit and track a high frequency signal to allow skiers lost in an avalanche or a crevasse to be found.

b

BASI - British Association of Snowsport Instructors.

binding - attaches boot to ski.

black run/piste - difficult, generally steeper than a red piste.

blood wagon - a stretcher on runners used by ski patrollers to carry injured skiers off the mountain.

blue run/piste - easy, generally wide with a gentle slope.

bubble ➥ 'gondola'.

button (or Poma) lift - for 1 person. Skis and boards run along the ground, whilst you sit on a small 'button' shaped seat.

c

cable car - a large box-shaped lift, running on a thick cable over pylons high above the ground, which carry up to 250 people per car.

carving - a recently developed turning technique used by skiers and boarders to make big, sweeping turns across the piste.

carving skis - shorter and fatter than traditional skis, used for carving turns.

chairlift - like a small and uncomfortable sofa, which scoops you and your skis off the ground and carries you up the mountain. Once on, a protective bar with a rest for your skis holds you in place. Can carry 2-6 people.

couloir - a 'corridor' between 2 ridges, normally steep and narrow.

crampons - spiked fittings attached to outdoor or ski boots to climb mountains or walk on ice.

d

draglift or (T-bar) - for 2 people. Skis and boards run on the ground, whilst you lean against a small bar.

drop-off - a sharp increase in gradient.

e

edge - the metal ridge on the border of each side of the ski.

f

FIS - Federation Internationale du Ski.

flat light - lack of contrast caused by shadow or cloud, making it very difficult to judge depth and distance.

freeriding, freeskiing - off-piste skiing.

freestyle - skiing involving jumps.

g

glacier - a slow-moving ice mass formed thousands of years ago and fed each year by fresh snow.

gondola (or bubble) - an enclosed lift, often with seats.

green run/piste - easiest, most gentle slope.

h

heliskiing - off-piste skiing on routes only accessible by helicopter.

high season - weeks when the resort is (generally) at full capacity.

i

glossary

itinerary route (yellow) - not groomed, maintained or patrolled. Generally more difficult, at least in part, than a black piste. Can be skied without a guide.

k

kicker - jump.

l

lambchop drag ➡ 'rope tow'.

ledgy - off-piste conditions in which there are many short, sharp drop-offs.

low season - beginning and end of the season and the least popular weeks in mid-January.

m

mid season - reasonably popular weeks in which the resort is busy but not full.

mogul - a bump, small or large, on or off piste. A large mogulled area is called a mogul field.

o

off-piste - the area away from marked, prepared and patrolled pistes.

p

parallel turn - skis turn in parallel.

piste - a ski run marked, groomed and patrolled, and graded in terms of difficulty (blue, red or black).

piste basher - a bulldozer designed to groom pistes by smoothing snow.

pisteur - a ski piste patroller.

Poma ➡ 'button lift'.

powder - fresh, unbashed or untracked snow.

r

raquettes ➡ 'snowshoes'.

red run/piste - intermediate, normally steeper than a blue piste, although a flatish piste may be a red because it is narrow, has a steep drop-off or because snow conditions are worse than on other pistes.

rope tow (or lambchop drag) - a constantly moving loop of rope with small handles to grab onto to take you up a slope.

s

schuss - a straight slope down which you can ski very fast.

seasonnaire - an individual who lives (and usually works) in a ski resort for the season.

skis - technology has changed in the last 10 years. New skis are now shorter and wider. When renting, you will be given a pair approx. 5-10cms shorter than your height.

ski patrol - a team of piste patrollers

skins - artificial fur attached to ski base, for ski touring.

snow-chains - chains attached to car tyres so that it can be driven (cautiously) over snow or ice.

snowshoes - footwear resembling tennis rackets which attach to shoes, for walking on soft snow.

spring snow - granular, heavy snow conditions common in late season (when daytime temperatures rise causing snow to thaw and re-freeze).

steeps - a slope with a very steep gradient.

t

T-bar ➡ 'draglift'.

w

white-out - complete lack of visibility caused by enveloping cloud cover.

index

a
accidents 123
accommodation 10, 18, 19, 26, 83, 120
- agencies 34
activities
- for children 115
- general 112
- snow 87
air travel 18, 19, 22, 122
airports 18, 19, 22, 122
apartments 34
après-ski 11, 90, 96, 104, 106, 110
- the best 91
ATMs 125
avalanches 124
b
bad weather 83
banks 125
bars 90, 91, 96, 104, 106, 110
beginners 37, 51
belleville valley 11, 72, 74, 76, 78
boarders 14, 38, 40, 41, 52, 53, 59, 61, 64, 79
board rental 40
bowling 112
brides-les-bains 35, 113
bus
- around méribel 25
- to méribel 20
c
cafés 91, 95, 109
camping 35
car hire 22, 122
car travel 20, 22, 122
chalets 14, 33, 120
chambéry 19, 22, 122
childcare 114
children 37, 43, 114
cinema 112
coach travel 20, 122
couloirs 64, 84
country survival 127
courchevel 1300
➥ le praz
courchevel 1550 69
courchevel 1650 67
courchevel 1850 63
crèche 114
cross-country skiing 87
currency 127
d
day-trips 113
disabled 43
DIY holidays 19
doctors 123
driving 20, 22, 122
e
eating out 11, 90, 92, 100, 102, 104, 108
- the best 91
email 117, 125
emergencies 123
equipment rental 39
ESF 41, 83, 87, 115
eurostar 22, 123
eurotunnel 20, 122
events 86
experts 52
f
families 15, 37, 114
ferries 20, 122
flights 18, 19, 22, 122
g
geneva 19, 22, 122
glaciers 78, 79, 80
grenoble 19, 22, 122
guides 45, 84
h
health 123
helicopter 122
heliskiing 87
hotels 26
- budget 31
- luxury 29
- mid-range 29
huskies 86, 87
i
ice skating 112
insurance 38, 39, 124
intermediates 52
internet 117, 125
itinerary routes 55, 59, 61
k
kids
➥ children
kindergarten 114
l
la masse 76
la tania 69
language 14
le praz 69
le rond-point 12, 26, 28, 50, 100, 114, 117
learning to ski 37, 51
les allues 12, 26, 51, 102
les menuires 74
lessons
- board 41
- children 43, 115
- skiing 41
lift passes 36, 115
lifts 49

index

lift tables
 ➥ inside back cover
lyon 19, 22, 122
m
maps
 ➥ contents
massage 113
maurienne valley 11, 78
méribel centre 12, 26, 28, 92, 112, 114
méribel village 12, 51, 104
minibus transfer 24, 123
money 127
mont du vallon 60
morel 12, 51, 100
mottaret 12, 51, 52, 106, 112, 114
mountain guides 45, 84
mountain huts 83, 85
moûtiers 20
n
nightclubs 99, 111
night-skiing 87, 115
non-skiers 37, 53
o
off-piste 11, 49, 55, 59, 61, 64, 68, 70, 73, 75, 77, 80, 84
off-piste equipment 40, 84
orelle 78
other resorts 25, 85
p
package holidays 18
parapenting 112
parc olympique 15, 112
parking 125
pharmacies 124
pistes 48
police 123
pralognan 85
r
rental
 - boards 40
 - boots 40
 - other equipment 40
 - skis 39
résidences 33
resort survival 125
resorts 90
restaurants 90, 92, 100, 102, 104, 108
 - the best 91
road travel
 - around méribel 25
 - to méribel 20
rules of conduct 124
s
safety 124
saulire 54
saunas 113
seasonnaires
 - before you go 116
 - once you're there 116
seniors 37
shopping 113, 126
ski areas 11
 ➥ contents
ski jump 86
ski maps
 ➥ inside back cover
ski rental 39
ski school 41, 115
ski touring 85
ski doos 87
skiing - where to start 50
snowboarders 14, 38, 40, 41, 52, 53, 59, 61, 64, 79
snowfall 13
snowparks 14, 38, 53, 59, 61, 64, 79
snowshoeing 87, 115
snowtrain 22, 123
squash 29
st. etienne 19, 22, 122
st. martin de belleville 72
suburbs, 12, 50, 100
suggested ski days 82
summer skiing 79
supermarkets 126
t
take-away food 95, 110
taxis 24, 126
temperatures 13
TGV 22, 123
tougnète 58
tour operators 18, 33, 120
tourist offices 126
train
 - long distance 20, 123
 - local 24
transfers 18, 19, 22, 122
travel
 - around méribel 25
 - to méribel 20
u
using the guide 4
using the maps 5
v
val thorens 78
volume of people 13
w
walking 37, 53
weather 13
weekends 18, 121

also available...

the snowmole guides to

chamonix mont-blanc
including argentière and full coverage of chamonix's 4 ski areas and the vallée blanche...

courchevel les 3 vallées
including 1850, 1650, 1550, le praz & la tania and full coverage of the 3 vallées ski area...

la plagne paradiski
including all 10 resorts and full coverage of the paradiski area and the vanoise express...

les arcs paradiski
including peisey-vallandry & arc 1950 and full coverage of the paradiski area and the vanoise express...

also available...

val d'isère espace killy
including st. foy and
full coverage of the espace
killy area...

verbier val de bagnes
including full coverage of the
4 vallées from verbier to
veysonnaz...

zermatt matterhorn
including full coverage of the
zermatt-cervinia ski area and the
matterhorn...

and coming soon the snowmole guides to...

st. anton arlberg
tignes espace killy
ski weekends
alpine secrets

& also the underground network

further information

accuracy & updates

We have tried our best to ensure that all the information included is accurate at the date of publication. However, because places change - improve, get worse, or even close - you may find things different when you get there. Also, everybody's experience is different and you may not agree with our opinion. You can help us, in 2 ways: by letting us know of any changes you notice and by telling us what you think - good or bad - about what we've written. If you have any comments, ideas or suggestions, please write to us at: snowmole, 45 Mysore Road, London, SW11 5RY or send an email to comments@snowmole.com

snowmole.com

Our website is intended as a compliment to our guides. Constantly evolving and frequently updated with news, you will find links to other wintersport related websites, information on our stockists and offers and the latest news about future editions and new titles. We also use our website to let you know of any major changes that occur after we publish the guides.

If you would like to receive news and updates about our books by email, please register your details at www.snowmole.com

order form

The snowmole guides are available from all major bookshops, wintersports retailers or direct from Qanuk Publishing & Design Ltd. To experience the Alps without leaving home have your next snowmole guide delivered to your door. To order send an email to sales@snowmole.com or fill in the form below and send it to us at Qanuk Publishing & Design Ltd, 45 Mysore Road, London, SW11 5RY

the snowmole guide to:	ISBN	quantity
chamonix mont blanc	0-9545739-3-5	--------------------------
courchevel les 3 vallées	0-9545739-5-1	--------------------------
la plagne paradiski	0-9545739-8-6	--------------------------
les arcs paradiski	0-9545739-7-8	--------------------------
méribel les 3 vallées	0-9545739-4-3	--------------------------
val d'isère espace killy	0-9545739-9-4	--------------------------
verbier val de bagnes	0-9545739-2-7	--------------------------
zermatt matterhorn	0-9545739-6-X	--------------------------

total: --------------------------
(£6.99 each, postage & packaging free)

I enclose a cheque for £
(made payable to Qanuk Publishing & Design Ltd)

name --
address --
postcode --
tel ---
email address ---
(please use block capitals)

Delivery will normally be within 14 working days. The availability and published prices quoted are correct at the time of going to press but are subject to alteration without prior notice. Please note that this service is only available in the UK.

Qanuk would like to keep you updated on new titles in the snowmole range or special offers. If you do not wish to receive such information please tick here ☐
Qanuk has a number of partners in the ski industry, and we may from time to time share your details with those partners if we think it might be of interest to you. If you do not wish us to share your details please tick here ☐

about you

Your comments, opinions and recommendations are very important to us. To help us improve the snowmole guides, please take a few minutes to complete this short questionnaire. Once completed please send it to us at Qanuk Publishing & Design Ltd.

name (Mr/Mrs/Ms) --
address --
postcode --
email address --
age --
occupation --

1. about your ski holiday (circle as appropriate)
how many days do you ski each year?
weekend/1 week/2 weeks/1 month/more
when do you book?
last-minute/1 month before/1-3 months before/3-6 months before/6+ months before
how do you book your holiday?
travel agent/mainstream tour operator/ski-specific tour operator/diy

2. about the snowmole guide
which title did you buy? --
where and when did you buy it? --
have you bought any other snowmole guides? --
if so, which one(s) --
how would you rate each section out of 5 (1 = useless, 5 = very useful)
getting started --
the skiing --
the resort --
the directory --
the maps --
what in particular made you buy this guide? --
----
do you have any general comments or suggestions? --
----
did you buy any other guides for your holiday? --
if yes, which one? --
Qanuk Publishing & Design Ltd may use information about you to provide you with details of other products and services, by telephone, email or in writing. If you do not wish to receive such details please tick here ☐

about us

snowmole / snṓmōl / n. & v. **1** a spy operating within alpine territory (esp. ski resorts) for the purpose of gathering local knowledge. **2** (in full **snowmole guide**) the guidebook containing information so gathered. v. research or compile or process intelligence on an alpine resort or surrounding mountainous area.

the authors

Isobel Rostron and Michael Kayson are snowsport enthusiasts who met while taking time out from real life to indulge their passion - Isobel to get it out of her system and Michael to ingrain it further. Michael's approach having won, they decided that a return to real life was overrated and came up with a cunning plan to make their passion their work. The result was snowmole.

acknowledgements & credits

None of this would have been possible without the help and support of many people:
Pascale Catalan & Jean-Marie Chöffel (Office de Tourisme de Méribel) for their assistance, Chris Herd & Vix Worrall for their incredibly generous hospitality, Mark Younger, Zoe Bannister, Richard Lumb and Sam from Ski Academy for their help in-resort, Maisie, Peter & Christine Rostron, Andrew Lilley, Angela & Julian Horne and Henry, Katie & Tom Fyson for their ongoing support.

The publishers would also like to thank the following for their kind permission to reproduce their photographs.
front cover: Office de Tourisme de Méribel
back cover: Office de Tourisme de Courchevel 1850 & Office de Tourisme de La Plagne
inside: title page, 10, 14, 15, 32, 33, 55, 61, 70, 82, 83, 84, 86, 87, 102 and 106 Office de Tourisme de Méribel and pages 64 & 85 Office de Tourisme de Courchevel 1850.
The remaining photographs are held in the publisher's own photo library and were taken by Isobel Rostron.

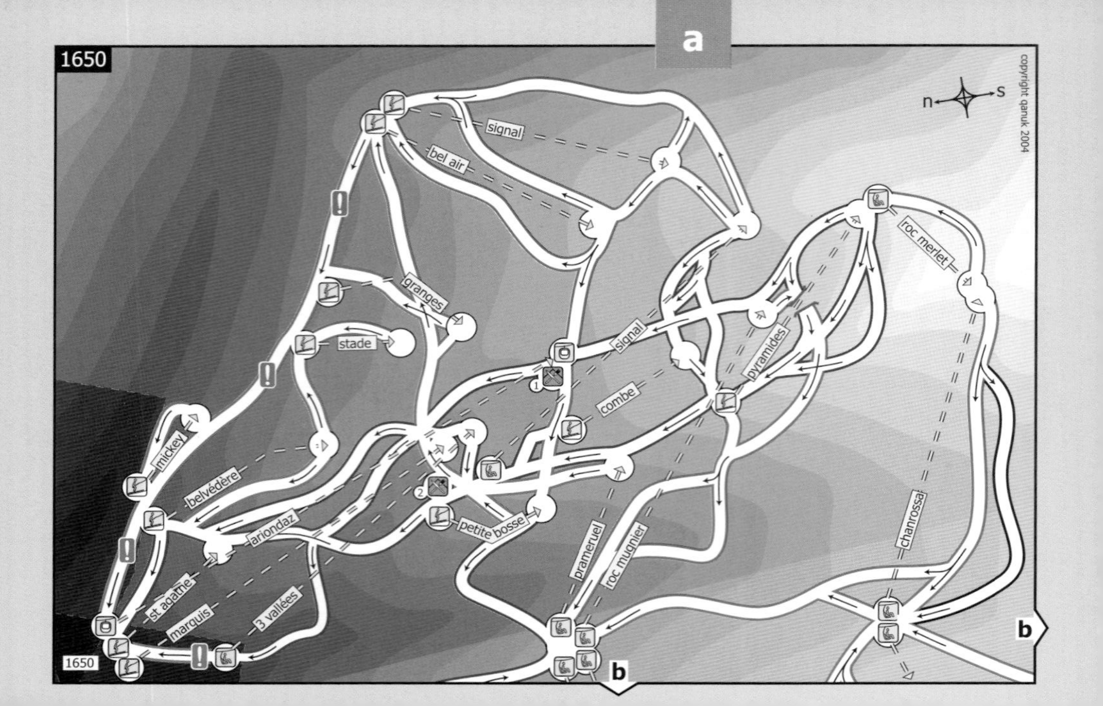

1650
a
copyright qanuk 2004
n
s
signal
bel air
granges
stade
mickey
belvédère
ariondaz
st agathe
marquis
3 vallées
signal
combe
pyramides
petite bosse
prameruel
roc mugnier
chanrossa
roc merlet
b
b
1650

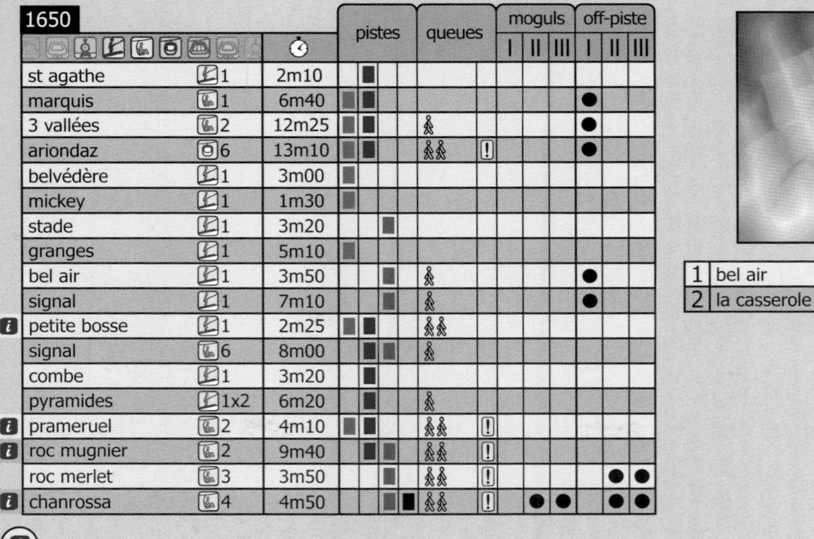

1650

1650		🕑	pistes				queues		moguls I	moguls II	moguls III	off-piste I	off-piste II	off-piste III
st agathe	1	2m10		■										
marquis	1	6m40	■	■								●		
3 vallées	2	12m25	■	■			🚶					●		
ariondaz	6	13m10	■	■			🚶🚶	!				●		
belvédère	1	3m00	■											
mickey	1	1m30	■											
stade	1	3m20			■									
granges	1	5m10	■											
bel air	1	3m50			■		🚶					●		
signal	1	7m10			■		🚶					●		
i petite bosse	1	2m25	■	■			🚶🚶							
signal	6	8m00		■	■		🚶							
combe	1	3m20		■										
pyramides	1x2	6m20		■			🚶							
i prameruel	2	4m10	■	■			🚶🚶	!						
i roc mugnier	2	9m40		■	■		🚶🚶	!						
roc merlet	3	3m50			■		🚶🚶	!					●	●
i chanrossa	4	4m50			■	■	🚶🚶	!		●	●		●	●

i	
prameruel/roc mugnier/ chanrossa	return from 1850 and the rest of the 3 vallées
petite bosse	use to return to 1850

1650

1	bel air
2	la casserole

a

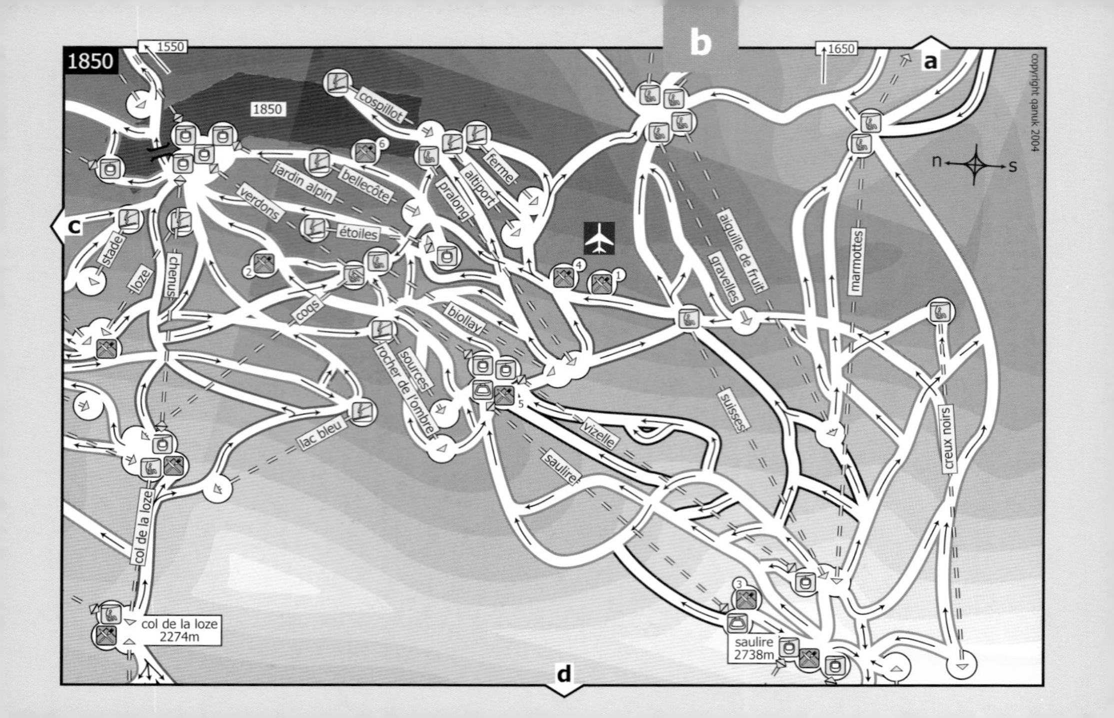
1850
1550
1650
b
a
c
d
n
s
copyright qanuk 2004
cospillot
1850
ferme
altiport
pralong
jardin alpin
bellecôte
verdons
étoiles
stade
loze
chenus
coqs
biollay
sources
rocher de l'ombre
lac bleu
vizelle
saulire
suisses
aiguille de fruit
gravelles
marmottes
creux noirs
col de la loze
col de la loze
2274m
saulire
2738m
1
2
3
4
5
6

1850		⏱	pistes				queues		moguls			off-piste		
									I	II	III	I	II	III
jardin alpin	6	9m00	■	■			3	!						
verdons	8	8m40	■				3	!						
bellecôte	1	4m20	■											
étoiles	1	3m20	■	■										
coqs	4	5m30	■	■			2	!				●	●	
cospillot	1	3m00		■										
pralong	6	7m30		■	■		2							
altiport	1	2m30		■										
ferme	1	1m30		■										
biollay	6	6m50		■	■		2							
sources	1	5m10	■											
rocher de l'ombre	1	7m00			■									
lac bleu	3	6m50		■								●	●	
saulire	160	4m20			■	■	2	!					●	●
vizelle	8	7m20			■	■	2							
suisses	4	6m40			■	■	2			●	●		●	
gravelles	4	7m20			■									
aiguille de fruit	3	7m20			■	■	2	!						
marmottes	6	5m25			■	■	2	!						
creux noirs	3	7m00			■								●	●

jardin alpin	3 stations, stays open after the pistes close for access to jardin alpin and for tobogganers

1850

1	cap horn
2	le chalet des pierres
3	le panoramic
4	le pilatus
5	l'arc en ciel
6	la bergerie

b

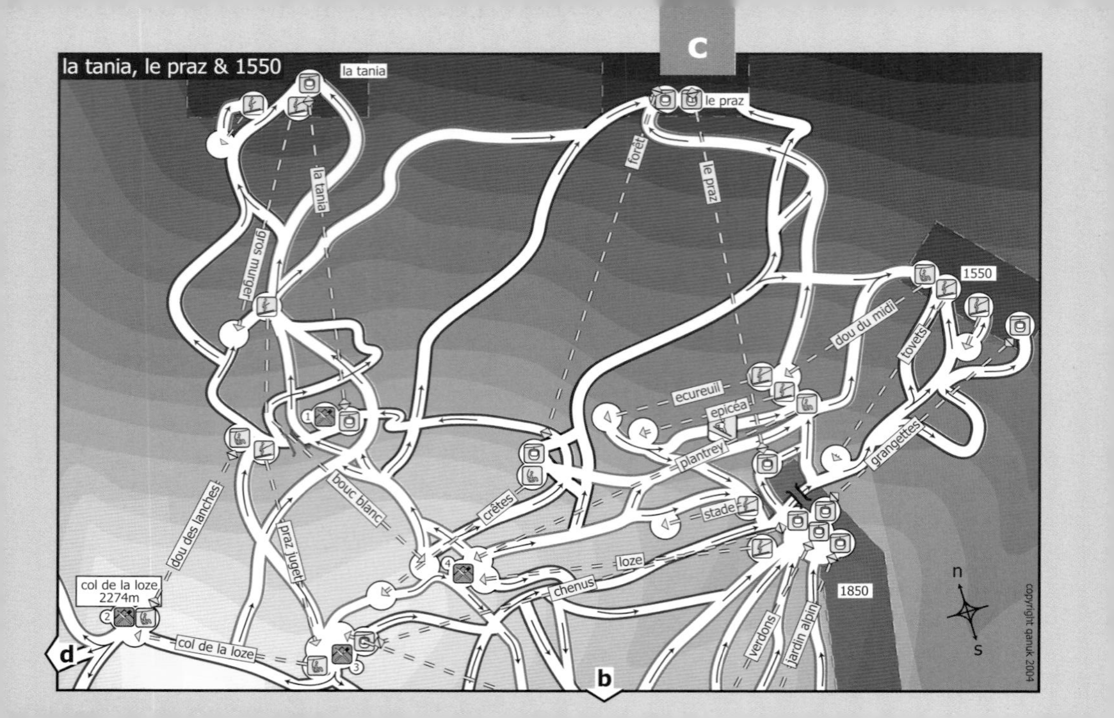

la tania, le praz & 1550
C
la tania
le praz
la tania
forêt
le praz
gros murger
1550
dou du midi
tovets
ecureuil
epicéa
plantrey
grangettes
bouc blanc
crêtes
stade
dou des lanches
praz juget
loze
chenus
col de la loze
2274m
1850
col de la loze
verdons
jardin alpin
n
s
d
b
1
2
3
4

la tania, le praz & 1550

	lift		⏱	pistes				queues		moguls I	moguls II	moguls III	off-piste I	off-piste II	off-piste III
	gros murger	1	7m00			■									
	la tania	12	7m45		■	■		🚶			●			●	
	forêt	4	9m00		■	■	■	🚶🚶	!		●			●	
	le praz	4	8m30	■		■		🚶🚶	!					●	
i	ecureuil	1	3m10	■				🚶🚶							
i	epicéa	1	3m00	■		■		🚶🚶							
	plantrey	4	7m00		■	■		🚶🚶	!		●			●	
	stade	1	4m00			■									
i	dou du midi	2	6m20			■									
i	tovets	1	7m30		■										
	bouc blanc	1	6m35	■	■	■		🚶						●	
i	dou des lanches	4	5m00		■	■	■	🚶🚶	!		●	●		●	●
i	col de la loze	2	6m45		■	■	■	🚶			●	●		●	●
	crêtes	3	6m05	■				🚶						●	
i	praz juget	1	5m00	■	■	■		🚶🚶	!		●			●	
	chenus	6	8m55	■	■	■		🚶🚶	!		●				
	loze	1	5m30	■	■	■									
	grangettes	4	7m30	■	■			🚶🚶	!						
	coqs	4	5m35	■	■	■		🚶🚶	!		●				

i	
ecureuil/epicéa	snowpark access
dou du midi/tovets	to be replaced winter 2005
col de la loze/dou des lanches	link to méribel
praz juget	téléski difficile

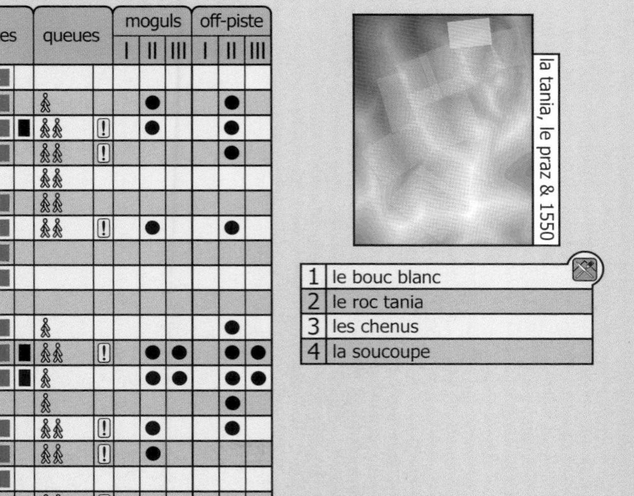
la tania, le praz & 1550

1	le bouc blanc
2	le roc tania
3	les chenus
4	la soucoupe

C

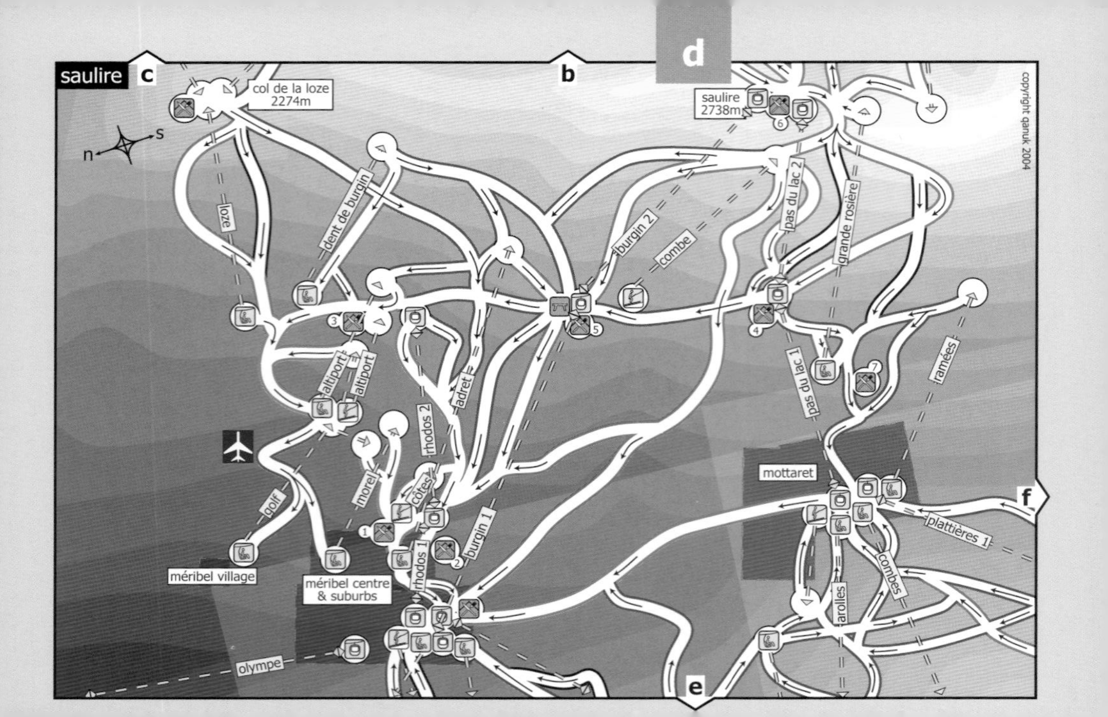
saulire
c
b
d
col de la loze
2274m
saulire
2738m
copyright qanuk 2004
n
s
loze
dent de burgin
burgin 2
combe
pas du lac 2
grande rosière
altiport
altiport
rhodos 2
adret
pas du lac 1
ramées
morel
côtes
golf
rhodos 1
burgin 1
mottaret
plattières 1
combes
arolles
méribel village
méribel centre
& suburbs
olympe
f
e
1
2
3
4
5
6
7

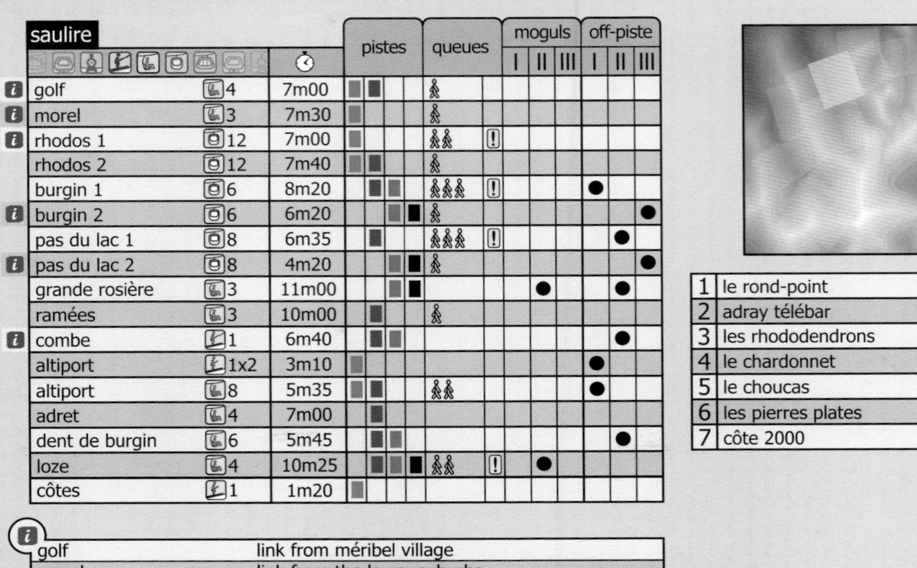

saulire

	lift	⏱	pistes				queues		moguls I	moguls II	moguls III	off-piste I	off-piste II	off-piste III
i golf	4	7m00	■	■			🚶							
i morel	3	7m30	■				🚶							
i rhodos 1	12	7m00	■				🚶🚶	!						
rhodos 2	12	7m40	■	■			🚶							
burgin 1	6	8m20		■	■		🚶🚶🚶	!				●		
i burgin 2	6	6m20			■	■	🚶							●
pas du lac 1	8	6m35		■			🚶🚶🚶	!					●	
i pas du lac 2	8	4m20			■	■	🚶							●
grande rosière	3	11m00			■	■				●			●	
ramées	3	10m00		■			🚶							
i combe	1	6m40		■	■								●	
altiport	1x2	3m10	■									●		
altiport	8	5m35	■	■			🚶🚶					●		
adret	4	7m00		■										
dent de burgin	6	5m45		■	■								●	
loze	4	10m25		■	■	■	🚶🚶	!		●				
côtes	1	1m20	■											

i	
golf	link from méribel village
morel	link from the lower suburbs
rhodos 1	link to le rond-point
burgin 2/pas du lac 2	courchevel valley access
combe	téléski difficile

saulire

1	le rond-point
2	adray télébar
3	les rhododendrons
4	le chardonnet
5	le choucas
6	les pierres plates
7	côte 2000

tougnète
e
d
f
g
n
s
copyright qanuk 2004
méribel centre & suburbs
olympe
stade
tougnète 1
roc de fer
plan de l'homme
arpasson
caves
olympic
cherferie
cherferie 2129m
roc de fer 2294m
tougnète
tougnète 2
table verte
tougnète 2434m
roc de tougne
mottaret
ramées
arolles
combes
plattières 1
1
2
3

tougnète

tougnète		⏱	pistes			queues		moguls I	moguls II	moguls III	off-piste I	off-piste II	off-piste III
roc de fer	4	9m15	■						●			●	●
stade	1	5m00	■		■								
plan de l'homme	6	10m40	■		■				●	●		●	
tougnète 1	6	10m40	■			🚶🚶🚶	!		●				
tougnète 2	6	6m15	■	■	■	🚶			●	●		●	
arpasson	1	4m40	■									●	
caves	1	4m00	■		■				●	●		●	
cherferie	1	5m25	■	■		🚶						●	
olympic	3	9m15	■		■				●			●	●
tougnète	1	6m25	■	■								●	

tougnète 2	links to st. martin & belleville valley, often closed in high winds
arpasson	snowpark access
cherferie	téléski difficile

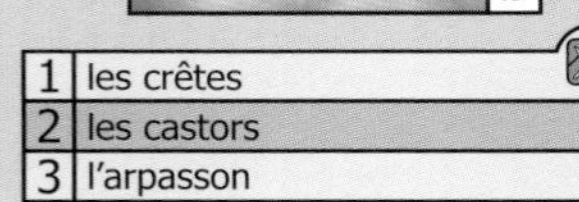

1	les crêtes
2	les castors
3	l'arpasson

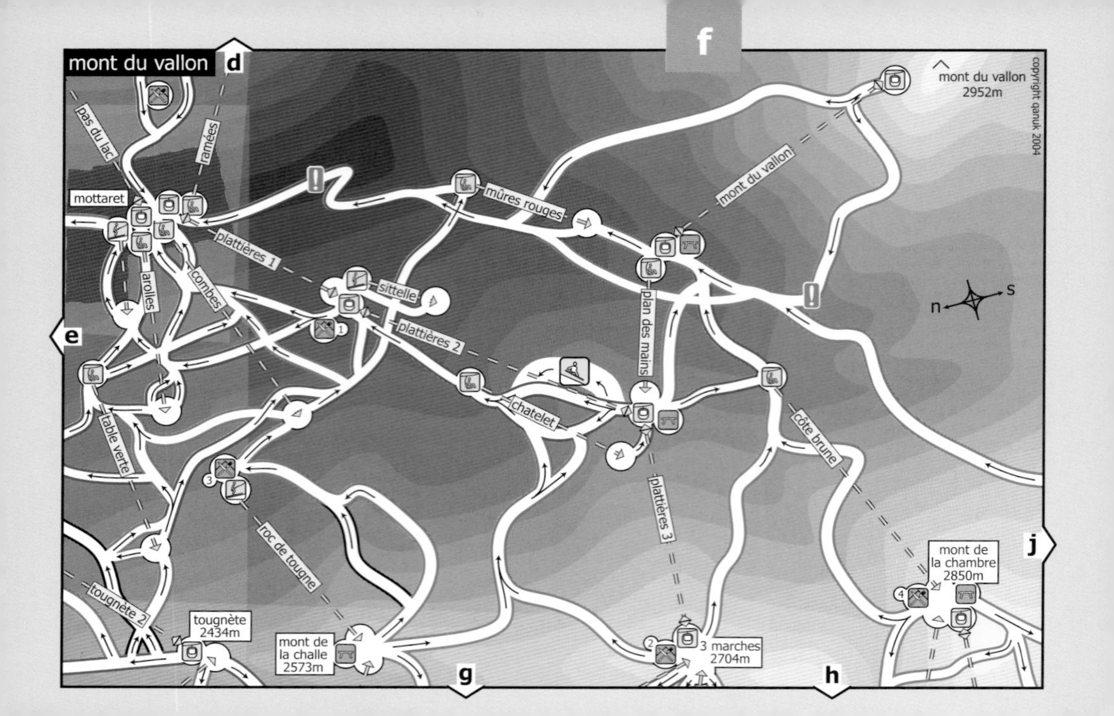
mont du vallon
f
d
e
g
h
j
mont du vallon
2952m
copyright qanuk 2004
n
s
mottaret
pas du lac
ramées
plattières 1
plattières 2
plattières 3
arolles
combes
sittelle
mûres rouges
mont du vallon
plan des mains
chatelet
côte brune
table verte
roc de tougne
tougnète 2
tougnète
2434m
mont de
la challe
2573m
3 marches
2704m
mont de
la chambre
2850m

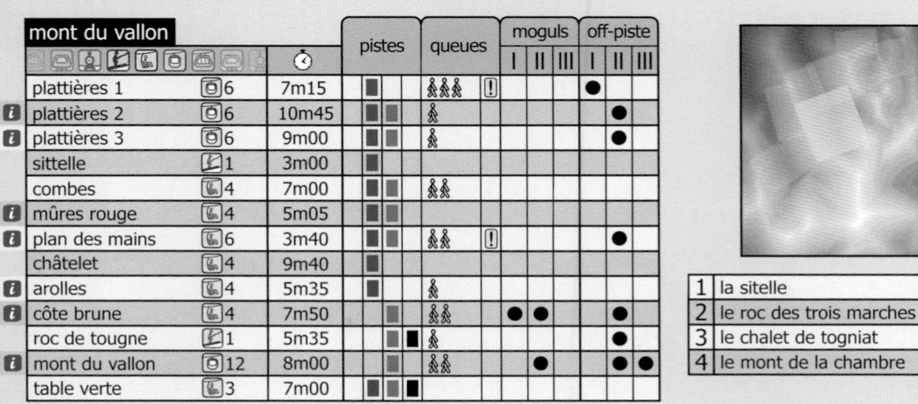

mont du vallon

lift		⏱	pistes			queues		moguls I	moguls II	moguls III	off-piste I	off-piste II	off-piste III
plattières 1	6	7m15	■			🚶🚶🚶	!				●		
plattières 2	6	10m45	■	■		🚶						●	
plattières 3	6	9m00	■	■		🚶						●	
sittelle	1	3m00	■										
combes	4	7m00	■	■		🚶🚶							
mûres rouge	4	5m05	■	■									
plan des mains	6	3m40	■	■		🚶🚶	!					●	
châtelet	4	9m40	■										
arolles	4	5m35	■			🚶							
côte brune	4	7m50		■		🚶🚶		●	●			●	
roc de tougne	1	5m35		■	■	🚶						●	
mont du vallon	12	8m00		■		🚶🚶			●			●	●
table verte	3	7m00	■	■	■								

plattières 2	exit at the top of plattières 2 to reach the côte brune chair and the link to val thorens
plattières 3	st. martin/les menuires access
mûres rouge	use to reach the plan des mains chair and avoid the 'ours' piste
plan des mains	return from val thorens/les menuires
arolles	use to reach mottaret accommodation at the end of the day
côte brune	val thorens access, often closed in high winds
mont du vallon	closes in high winds

mont du vallon

1	la sitelle
2	le roc des trois marches
3	le chalet de togniat
4	le mont de la chambre

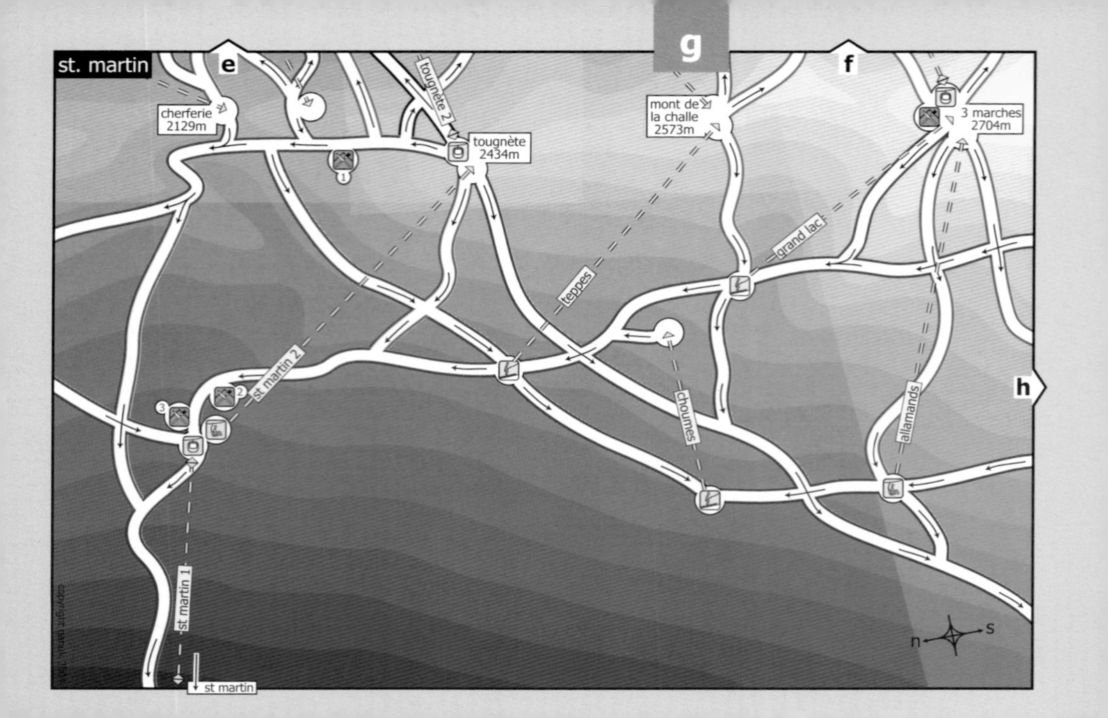
st. martin
e
g
f
h
cherferie
2129m
tougnète 2
tougnète
2434m
mont de
la challe
2573m
3 marches
2704m
grand lac
teppes
st martin 2
choumes
allamands
st martin 1
st martin
1
2
3
n
s

st. martin

lift		time	pistes		queues		moguls I	moguls II	moguls III	off-piste I	off-piste II	off-piste III
st. martin 1	8	12m40	■			(!)				●		
st. martin 2	4	8m40	■	■							●	
teppes	1	8m15		■								
choumes	1	4m55	■									
grand lac	1	4m30	■	■								
allamands	3	6m40	■	■								

st. martin 2	link to méribel valley
teppes	most direct lift to pistes above mottaret
choumes/grand lac	to be replaced by a 6-man chairlift winter 2005

1	les crêtes
2	le corbeleys
3	le chardon bleu

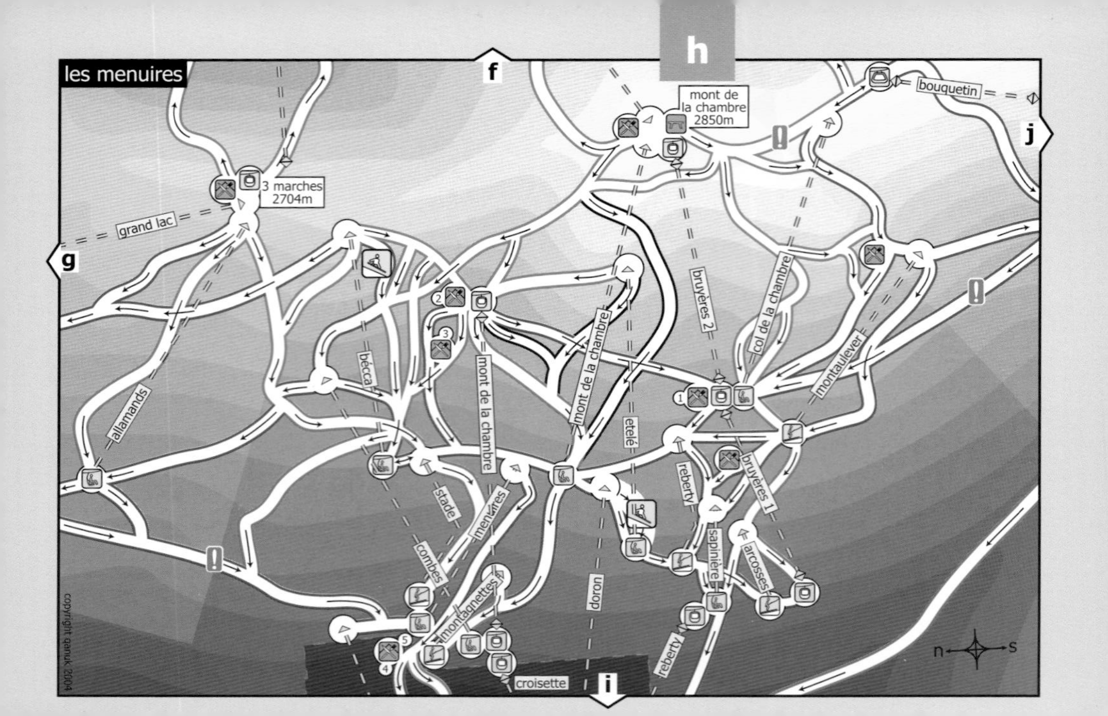
les menuires
h
f
g
j
i
mont de
la chambre
2850m
3 marches
2704m
bouquetin
grand lac
allamands
bécca
mont de la chambre
mont de la chambre
bruyères 2
col de la chambre
montaulever
etelé
reberty
bruyères 1
stade
menuires
combes
montagnettes
doron
sapinière
arcosses
reberty
croisette
n
s
copyright qanuk 2004

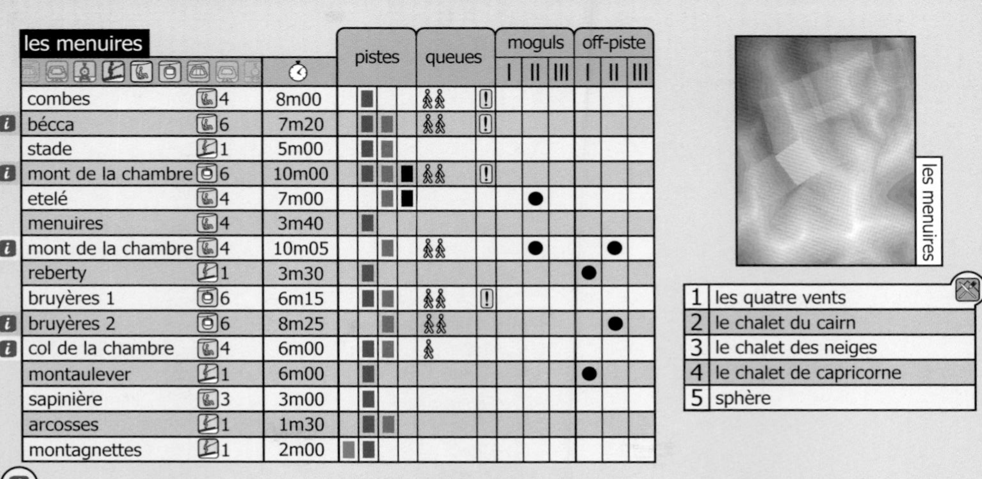

les menuires

		⏱	pistes				queues		moguls I	moguls II	moguls III	off-piste I	off-piste II	off-piste III
combes	4	8m00		■			👤👤	(!)						
bécca	6	7m20		■	■		👤👤	(!)						
stade	1	5m00		■	■									
mont de la chambre	6	10m00		■	■	■	👤👤	(!)						
etelé	4	7m00			■	■				●				
menuires	4	3m40		■										
mont de la chambre	4	10m05			■		👤👤			●			●	
reberty	1	3m30		■								●		
bruyères 1	6	6m15		■	■		👤👤	(!)						
bruyères 2	6	8m25			■		👤👤						●	
col de la chambre	4	6m00		■	■		👤							
montaulever	1	6m00		■								●		
sapinière	3	3m00		■										
arcosses	1	1m30		■	■									
montagnettes	1	2m00	■	■										

i	
bécca	return to the méribel valley by the roc des 3 marches
mont de la chambre/ bruyères 2/col de la chambre	return to the méribel valley by the mont de la chambre

les menuires

1	les quatre vents
2	le chalet du cairn
3	le chalet des neiges
4	le chalet de capricorne
5	sphère

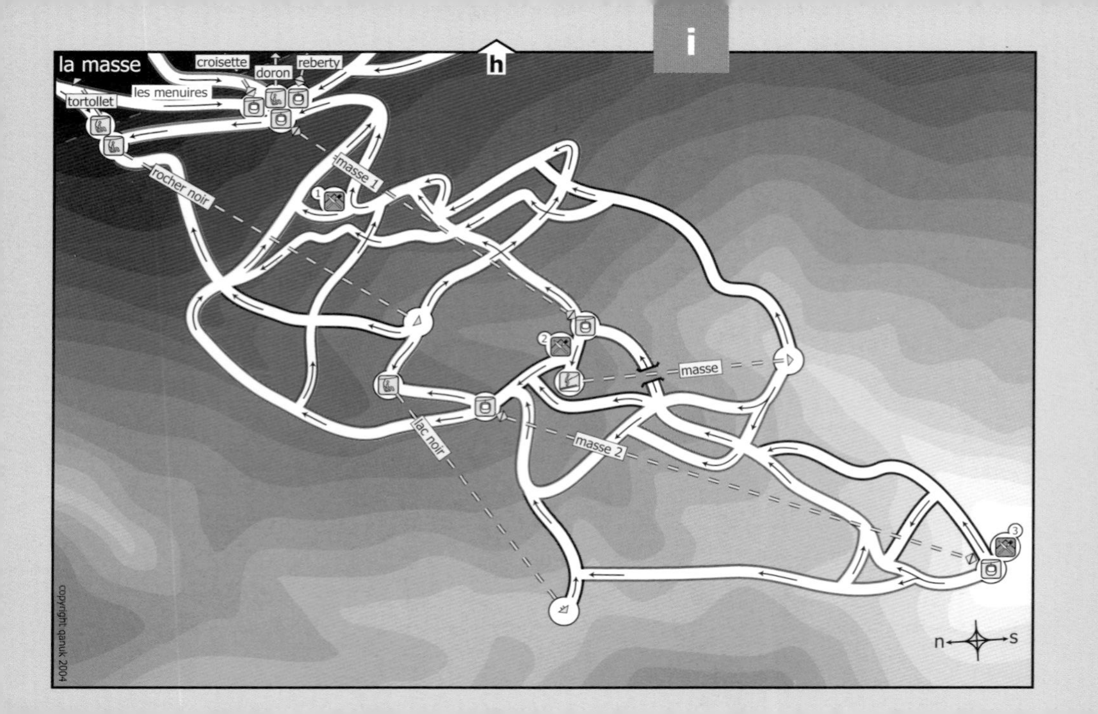

la masse
croisette
doron
reberty
h
i
les menuires
tortollet
masse 1
rocher noir
1
2
3
masse
lac noir
masse 2
n
s

la masse

lift		⏱	pistes				queues		moguls I	moguls II	moguls III	off-piste I	off-piste II	off-piste III
masse 1	(gondola) 12	6m40			■	■	🚶🚶					●		
masse 2	(gondola) 12	10m55			■	■	🚶			●			●	●
rocher noir	(chairlift) 3	7m00		■	■	■			●				●	
masse (i)	(drag lift) 1	3m20			■	■								
lac noir (i)	(chairlift) 3	11m50				■				●			●	●
doron	(chairlift) 4	5m10		■			🚶🚶							
croisette	(gondola)	3m00		■			🚶🚶							
reberty	(gondola)	3m40		■										
tortellet	(chairlift) 3	5m20		■										

i

masse	often closed
lac noir	cold on snowy/windy days

la masse

1	les 3V
2	les roches blanches
3	le panoramic

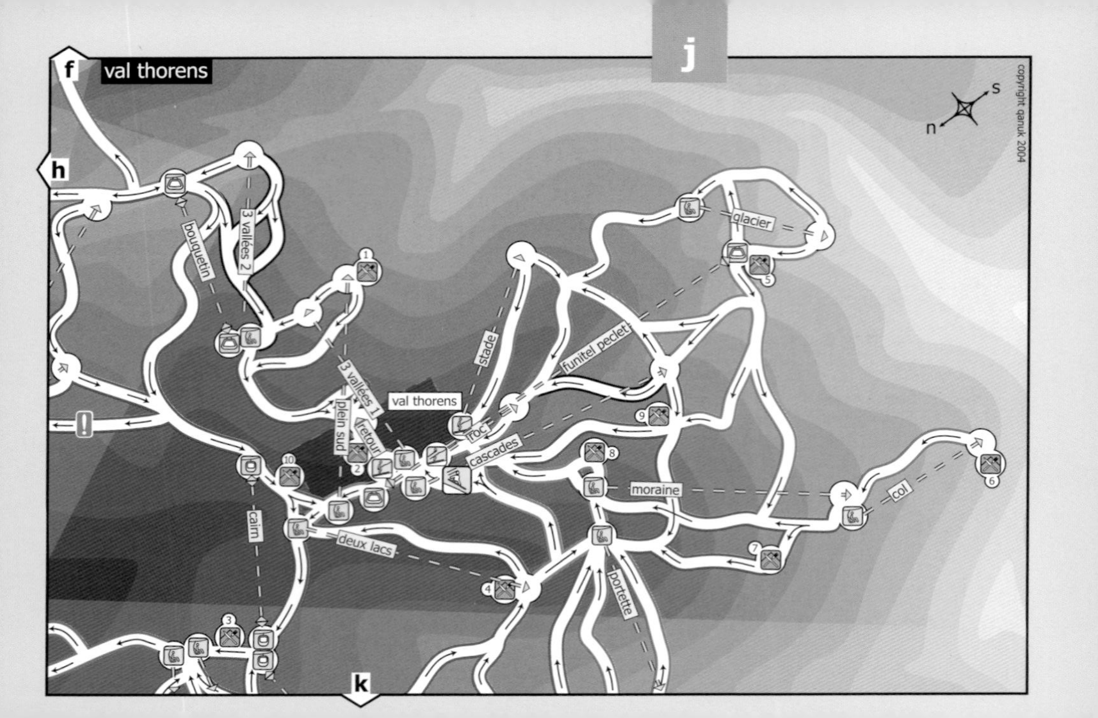
j
f
val thorens
h
copyright qanuk 2004
s
n
bouquetin
3 vallées 2
1
glacier
5
stade
funitel peclet
3 vallées 1
val thorens
plein sud
retour
roc
cascades
9
8
10
2
moraine
col
6
cairn
deux lacs
7
4
portette
3
k

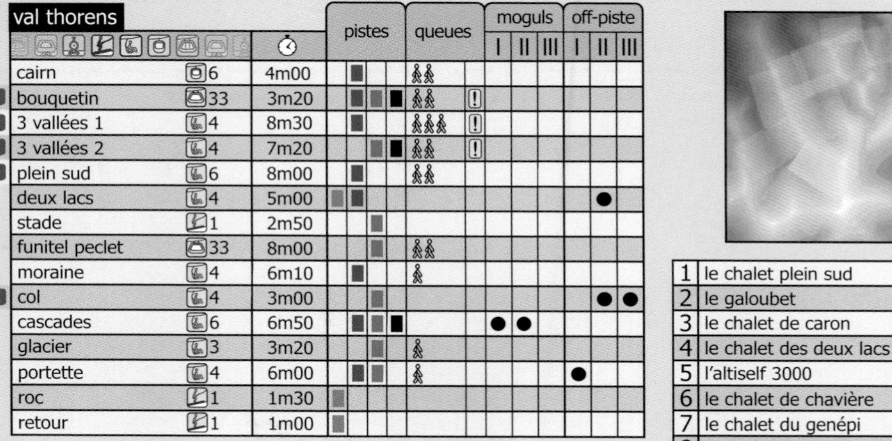

val thorens

		⏱	pistes				queues		moguls I	moguls II	moguls III	off-piste I	off-piste II	off-piste III
cairn	6	4m00		■			🚶🚶							
bouquetin	33	3m20		■	■	■	🚶🚶	!						
3 vallées 1	4	8m30		■			🚶🚶🚶	!						
3 vallées 2	4	7m20			■	■	🚶🚶	!						
plein sud	6	8m00		■			🚶🚶							
deux lacs	4	5m00	■	■									●	
stade	1	2m50			■									
funitel peclet	33	8m00			■		🚶🚶							
moraine	4	6m10		■			🚶							
col	4	3m00			■								●	●
cascades	6	6m50		■	■	■			●	●				
glacier	3	3m20			■		🚶							
portette	4	6m00		■	■		🚶					●		
roc	1	1m30	■											
retour	1	1m00	■											

plein sud	alternative route back to méribel valley
3 vallées 1	expect long queues at the end of the day
bouquetin/3 vallées 2	links to méribel valley
col	rarely open

val thorens

1	le chalet plein sud
2	le galoubet
3	le chalet de caron
4	le chalet des deux lacs
5	l'altiself 3000
6	le chalet de chavière
7	le chalet du genépi
8	le chalet du thorens
9	le bar de la marine
10	l'oxalys

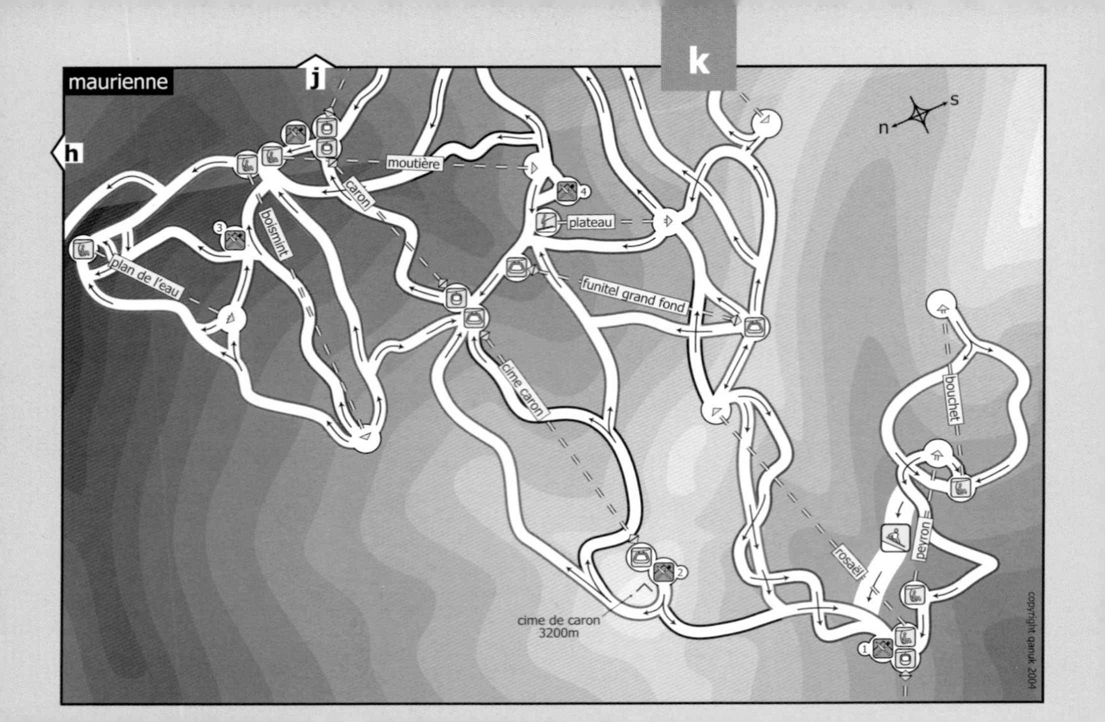
maurienne
h
j
n
s
moutière
caron
boismint
plan de l'eau
plateau
funitel grand fond
cime caron
bouchet
peyron
rosaël
cime de caron
3200m
1
2
3
4
copyright qanuk 2004

maurienne

lift		⏱	pistes				queues		moguls I	moguls II	moguls III	off-piste I	off-piste II	off-piste III
plan de l'eau	4	9m20		■	■							●		
boismint	4	7m10		■	■							●		
caron	6	7m20		■			🚶🚶	!						
cime caron	150	4m40			■	■	🚶🚶	!					●	●
plateau	1	3m30		■										
funitel grand fond	33	8m20		■	■		🚶🚶						●	●
rosaël	4	9m10		■	■	■	🚶						●	●
peyron	4	11m40		■						●			●	
bouchet	4	10m00			■								●	●
moutière	6	8m10		■		■	🚶🚶		●	●			●	

i	
cime caron	closes in high winds, link to 4th valley
funitel grand fond	link to 4th valley
rosaël	return from 4th valley
peyron	boardercross access

1	plan bouchet refuge
2	l'étape 3200
3	le chalet de deux ours
4	la moutière

ski area key

courchevel

a - courchevel 1650
b - courchevel 1850
c - la tania, le praz & 1550

méribel

d - saulire
e - tougnète
f - mont du vallon

belleville

g - st. martin de belleville
h - les menuires
i - la masse
j - val thorens
k - maurienne

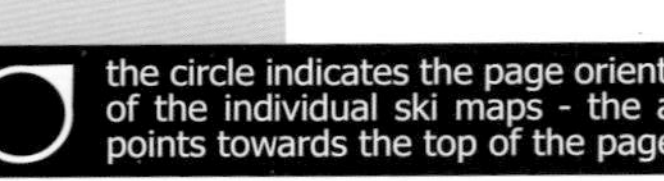